ALONE WITH GOD

A Guide for a Personal Retreat

Ron DelBene
with Herb Montgomery

Harper & Row, Publishers, San Francisco
Cambridge, Hagerstown, New York, Philadelphia
London, Mexico City, São Paulo, Singapore, Sydney

Other books by the authors:
The Breath of Life: Discovering Your Breath Prayer
The Hunger of the Heart

Cover design: Art Direction, Inc.

The Scripture quotations in this publication are from the *Revised Standard Version Common Bible,* copyright © 1973 by the Division of Christian Education of the National Council of the Churches of Christ in the U.S.A. Used by permission.

Library of Congress Catalog Card Number: 84-60810

ISBN: 0-86683-856-2

Printed in the United States of America

5   4   3   2

Contents

To my father and mother

Introduction

"How do you write a book *with* someone?" people often ask. "It ain't easy!" I reply, and that gets a smile because I've given the expected answer. After all, how could any two people work on such an extended project without having heated disagreements?

It's true that when friends create a book together there is a lot of give and take, but the resolutions Ron and I reach are not compromises in which either of us must "give up" something. That's because our goal has always been to communicate his ideas as clearly as possible. We try to speak directly to readers and avoid the theological talk of textbooks, believing that spiritual growth is much more dependent on what you do than what you know. Having a shared goal enables Ron and me to look in an objective way at what he writes and then decide together what needs to be done. I also think that our very different backgrounds help us to cooperate and collaborate without competition.

Ron's Southern home is far from my home near Minneapolis. He is ordained; I am not. He is comfortable speaking to large groups; I am more at ease facing ideas alone at my word processor. Our differences enable us to write from a broader and more balanced perspective than either of us could alone.

In fifteen years of watching Ron move from the business world to be ordained and go on to serve his own parish, I've been impressed by his commitment to erase that line that so often separates what one knows from what one does. Ron practices—as well as teaches and preaches—spiritual growth. (He is quick to admit, however, that preaching

1

sometimes comes easier than practicing!)

Ron's family includes his wife, Eleanor, and their two children, Paul and Anne. Eleanor has a special interest in spirituality as well as in holistic health and healing. In her work, she stresses the importance of realizing that being a whole and well person requires a concern not only for the physical and mental sides of ourselves but also for the emotional and spiritual dimensions.

The DelBenes are at home in the rolling hills northeast of Birmingham, Alabama. Along their road there's just enough distance between the houses to give you the feeling that you're in a rural area. Downhill from their house—at the end of a gravel path—is the Hermitage, a small retreat house hidden in a woods of pines and other trees.

Much of Ron's writing is done alone at the Hermitage, where there is no phone to interrupt him. It's a contemplative place to which others come for a few days or even weeks to be alone with God. In this sense, the Hermitage is more an experience than a place. People who stay there work under Ron and Eleanor's direction and are encouraged to keep journals. These journals become personal and powerful works that reflect what happens when we let the Lord enter more fully into our lives. We're especially thankful that people have allowed Ron to use their journal entries to give others a sense of what can happen when you make the choice to be alone with God.

The last time I stayed in the Hermitage, I was touched by the silent aloneness and recognized how necessary this aloneness is. Calm times in our lives are like islands from which we are free to explore. In the silence, we reach out and God truly does speak to us, but what is said applies to *both* our God-relationship *and* the busy life we've momentarily left behind. For me, perspective is restored.

I always leave silent time eager to talk, and talk is one of the delightful elements of mealtime with the DelBenes, who make me feel like one of the family whenever I visit.

Everyone—including the kids—gets involved in the big kitchen. Two cats come begging and get shooed away to eat their own food. There's a jumble of talk that is like family music we all enjoy. Children are hungry, so our prayers are short! This is not a pious or pompous gathering. This is a family that laughs and interrupts and mixes concerns about schoolwork and computers with jokes and challenges to play a new boardgame after supper. (Beginning with the days when they were youngsters, Anne and Paul have assured me I'll love their newest game and find it easy. So I play, and they whip me with the glee that children revel in when they outwit an adult.)

Ron is part of a family that is pulled in many directions the way all families are, and he's still learning how to make the most of those hours when everyone can be together. Each of his books speaks to readers in a gentle way that reflects the best of what all of us hope to become, wherever we live. As a pastor, he's well aware that we're all in the midst of change. His work reflects the Christian hope that through our own change process we will come to know more of ourselves and more of God. In his books, Ron never asks us to try something he hasn't tried himself, and his invitation to others to take responsibility for their spiritual growth is a sincere and loving one.

While working on this third book with Ron, I realized that the God he believes in is much quicker to smile than to frown and always extends a helping, loving hand our way. All we need do is reach out and accept it. *Alone with God* is meant to make that acceptance easier for those of us who lead busy lives and often feel the need for a little help in continuing our spiritual journey.

Herb Montgomery

Part One

Getting Ready

Chapter 1

Alonetime

Beginnings

We were sitting around a fireplace quietly sharing thoughts about the retreat for which we had all gathered. Although we were strangers, there was within the group an obvious feeling of warmth and support, the warmth and support that create the trust people need to feel in order to allow others into their private thoughts.

Susan was the first to speak up. "It's amazing," she said, "that I'd be afraid to be alone with God!" Susan was forty-one, married, and the mother of a teenage son. I knew it had been hard for her (as it was for the others) to find the time to get away for this retreat. Her admission of fear completely changed the level of our conversation, bringing forth deeper feelings about what it's like to reach out alone to God. Bill, a young lawyer active in community affairs, echoed Susan's concerns as he admitted, "Whenever I think I'd want to take some time just to be alone with God, I immediately wonder, What would I *do?*"

The conversation that evening confirmed everything I had been hearing through the years in other retreats all across the country as well as in private spiritual direction sessions with people who come to stay at the Hermitage, where I do much of my work. It's certainly no longer a secret that *many of us find it extremely difficult to be alone with God because we're not sure what to do and have no idea what to expect.*

The uncertainty we feel is not something we like to

admit, but it does exist and is a definite barrier that anyone seriously concerned about personal spiritual growth must break through. This book is my response to the many people who want to be alone with God but are at a loss as to what to do. It is especially for women like Martha and men like Bradley who have shared so generously with me. Martha is a middle-aged woman living in a small Southern town. She told me, "I have no one to direct me in my alone time. If only there were someone nearby, or something to guide me." Bradley expressed much the same sentiment in a city hundreds of miles away. He said, "Even though there are a lot of resources, there are times when I'd like to just take my Bible and go off for a couple of hours or even a day—in the woods, at the beach, or just in the church. But I'd feel foolish. I need some direction."

It used to be that people wanted to be alone with God in some quiet setting exclusively for what we called "spiritual reasons." While these spiritual reasons still exist, during the past ten years or so we've all become aware of our physical, mental, and emotional needs for renewal as well. In fact, there is one Midwestern college that won't grant a degree to anyone who hasn't completed work in at least one course whose express purpose is to help students understand their need for self re-creation.

Many of the hurried, hassled people I counsel are concerned about their inability to slow down, reflect, exercise, eat better, pay attention to their environment. Those who decide to learn how to spend a little time alone with God soon realize it's foolish to try to "get right" with God without considering their whole life and the need to correct *whatever* is out of balance.

While there's a definite spiritual hunger, which I described in *The Hunger of the Heart,* many people are yearning to put not only one room but their entire house in order. I believe this is best done when we're attentive to God's power in our lives. The place to begin is a setting within which we can admit our fears and be alone with

God. Then we'll recognize that God's power and Spirit call us to be whole people and there is no reason to be afraid of drawing closer to God, who is love. Jesus will say to us as he so often said to his followers, "Do not be afraid."

As we begin to look at this venture, it's important to realize that at least part of the personal confusion we feel is created by messages promoting the belief that being alone and being lonely are the same experience. Advertising, for example, plays on the idea that if we use the right toothpaste, smoke the right cigarette, and wear the right clothes, we'll have lots of friends, be the center of attention, and be neither alone nor lonely. Such messages may be good for the economy, but they also create misunderstandings. Being alone and being lonely are not the same. It's true that we may be lonely when we're alone, but we can experience that same isolation in a crowd even though we're wearing the latest fashions or using the right toothpaste. Lonely is what we feel—an emotion, an inner experience. Alone is what we are—a physical placement, an outer condition.

In discussing being alone with God, I consider the word "alone" to involve the willing placement of ourselves in a setting where we're free of distraction and more open to realize that we can go in the direction God intends. Alone, in this sense, is a positive experience, a time when we begin to see the depth of ourselves. We've all known people who can "put on a happy face" whenever they feel the situation calls for it. Such people may be good actors, but they're really wearing masks. When we're alone with God, we take off all masks and consciously intend to have our outside match our inside. This is a positive step toward becoming what we're called by God to be!

Being alone with God will not dispel lonely feelings immediately. But it will give us the inner strength we need to seek worthwhile relationships, build friendships, and involve ourselves in activities that give us satisfaction and a sense of wholeness. Eventually such purposeful involvement leaves us with little time for feeling lonely.

Attentiveness

Did you ever say something to your boss or spouse or child and feel as if you were talking to a brick wall? If so, you knew that that person wasn't paying attention to what you had to say. There was talk but no communication. It's somewhat the same when God speaks to us directly and through others and we fail to pay attention. How many times have we missed opportunities of ministry or service to those around us because we weren't attentive? When we complain about not feeling God's presence, perhaps we're like the unlistening brick wall that so infuriates us.

Being attentive is a key to spending time alone with God and recognizing that we're growing because of God's presence. Although we can be open and attentive right at home, many people find it easier at first to seek harmony with God in other surroundings. Getting away from our normal, everyday activities makes us much more alert. In that heightened state, we look and listen with increased potential, seeing and hearing with great expectations. We're truly attentive and more likely to discern what we must do to be more in touch with God and to understand God's purpose for us.

Silence: An Enemy, or a Friend?

Did you ever get the "silent treatment" as a child or as an adult? This treatment is often used by people who want to hurt us. In this instance, silence becomes something we dread; silence, as well as the person who causes it, may become an enemy. In other circumstances, silence is equated with nondoing, nonproductivity, and sometimes evil. Learning to be still (silent) in God's presence may be very difficult for us if we view purposeful quiet negatively, as Mike did.

Mike was an overscheduled dentist whose days included nonstop activity both in and out of the office. He
was thirty-six when he came to the Hermitage to spend
four days in solitude. This is what he wrote in his journal
the first evening he spent without the usual company of
radio, TV, or people with whom he might talk:

> Here I am. For nearly four months, I've been looking
> forward to coming here and having some time alone
> with God, but I'm suddenly filled with a great deal of
> apprehension. What will I do?
>   I realize that I'm a doer, and here all I have to do is
> be. I'm not a be-er. (But I'd love a beer!)
>   I'm really afraid.

Why would a grown man be apprehensive about spending four days in silence, solitude, and prayer? Because, as
a do-er, Mike saw silence as nondoing and nonproductive.
As a consequence, he felt powerless. What was expected?
He didn't know. Deep down it's a control issue. We want to
be in control rather than giving over our power, our control, to God.

Mike's beer pun is significant because it points out how,
when we face a difficult situation regarding growth, spiritual or otherwise, we often seek some diversion. We use
food, drink, music, sports, clothes, and sometimes even
religion to avoid paying attention to God's personal call.

As a child growing up in Ohio, I often went to a lake
cottage with my parents. For them, it was wonderful
because there was no phone, no TV, no mail, and a radio
that was to be turned on only for emergency weather
reports. The place seemed dull to me, especially the first
few hours, but then as I put my attention to the task, I
found ways to entertain myself. Since then the "lake-
time" of my youth has become a pleasant memory, because
now, as a pastor and parent, I often find my life run by the
telephone and the mail. I might add the children's soccer
games, musical events, and family discussions of what to

watch on TV. Now I welcome the silence I didn't used to appreciate. It's no enemy.

To respect the true value of silence, we need only recall those moments when we've been touched in soundless but wondrous ways. Rocking a child to sleep, quietly stroking a favored pet, the presence of a dear friend—these are comforting experiences that require no words to be appreciated. Our presence speaks to child, pet, and friend alike. God's presence speaks just as clearly when we're attentive, but in a busy society it's all too easy to ignore our spiritual-listening ability.

I remember the days when I worked out of Minneapolis, traveling crowded freeways morning and night and shuttling back and forth across the country by plane. It seemed as if I was never away from noise. Then I took a vacation in Canada's Sibley Provincial Park on the north side of Lake Superior. I had forgotten what quiet can mean. But quiet was there. Along with sky blues and earth greens, it refreshed my senses and opened me to the possibilities of "hearing the silence." Hiking along a nature trail, I recognized how the steady pace of business and city life can deaden our capacity to listen for and recognize what is sacred.

What about you? Are you ready to let go of some of the busy-ness and pressures of your life and rediscover silence? You can begin with as few as two hours and build up to a weekend when you're ready for it. Come, my friend. Let's journey a little further spiritually by taking time alone with God.

Chapter 2

Finding Space

There's a need within us to define and defend our space. We see this even in young children who wall off an area with blocks or chairs and throw tantrums if anyone intrudes. They turn a large cardboard box into a house that no one may enter unless invited. Older children hang signs on their bedroom doors, signs that range from serious—Private, Keep Out—to humorous—Disaster Zone, Enter at Your Own Risk.

As adults, we lay individual claim to some part of the house. It may be a darkroom, a sewing room, a workbench area of the basement, or even a shed in the back yard. At the very least, we set aside some chair. Other family members tend to respect this staking out of territory because they recognize that every person has the right to say, "That's mine!" Although it may appear to be a selfish action, we each need to have our own space in both a secular and a religious sense. We must have a place to which we can retreat to be alone with God, and we need the assurance from others that that place will be respected. Whether the space is large or small doesn't matter. What is important is knowing that space is mine when I need it or want it.

When we purposely set out to create a space rather than just take over whatever is available, we design the area to fit our specific needs. When we build a house, the garage—which is to be mainly a storage area—receives less attention than the den or living room in which we expect to spend more time. If you've ever looked through an empty house with the intention of renting or buying, you probably recall how you immediately began thinking what purposes you'd assign to various rooms and how you'd place your furniture. What the last person used as a child's bedroom, you might envision as an office or study.

For our time alone with God, we want to be in an environment that's already set up to help us focus on the task at hand, or one that we can easily adapt to that purpose. Most people find it extremely difficult to feel peaceful and reflective when the surroundings are jarring to their senses. So let's look first to the church building and see whether there might already be a space that suits our needs.

More and more churches are setting aside places for individuals seeking quiet time for reflection and meditation. One church I visited had transformed a junky, little-used storage room into a "retreat room." The floor was carpeted, attractive artwork hung on the walls, and a small altar had been constructed as a focal point. In addition, a desk and a chair were provided for reading and writing, and a cot stood along one wall for anyone needing rest. People who want to use the room call the church office to make a reservation and then stop by at the appointed time to pick up the key. Another church has about the same arrangement, but it has provided an under-the-counter refrigerator so that people who want to stay alone all day, or through mealtime, have a place to store the necessary food.

A somewhat different approach is offered by a church that has a "still place" with a small library of inspirational tapes and books people may listen to or read.

Another church has worked from a thematic approach, basing the decor of the meditation space on scripture. Church members designed and painted a large burning bush on one wall. The bush is the focal point of the room that everyone refers to as "holy ground."

Using a room within their local church is especially convenient for people who do not like to be alone without someone nearby. Such rooms are becoming more common but aren't yet widely available. If your church doesn't have a private prayer room, discuss the idea wth friends and see whether it's something to pursue.

Your home is, of course, the next place to consider. Although very few of us can reserve an entire room for our spiritual pursuits, most of us can set aside some part of the house or apartment where we can be alone and undisturbed for the time we'll need. Unfortunately, there are drawbacks to making even a two-hour retreat at home. In familiar surroundings, we tend to think and act in our old familiar ways and are perhaps less open to new possibilities than we should be. Being aware of this, we'll want to make a commitment and stick to it. It's definitely best to have the place to yourself. To avoid interruptions and distractions, you'll want to quiet the doorbell with a note such as "Do not disturb until (time)" and stop the ringing phone. You can unplug the phone, connect it to an answering machine if you have one, or simply turn it to the gentlest ring and muffle it with pillows.

If you favor getting out of the house for a couple hours to be alone with God in nature, consider a park, a beach, a forest, the desert, or whatever nearby place inspires you. *It's important, however, that you feel physically secure in the setting you select* and as sure as you possibly can be that no one and nothing will intrude upon your time.

It's also possible to combine alone time with a day or two of rest and recreation. Expenses can be kept to a minimum by renting a cabin during the off season. Large hotel and motel complexes often have "weekend specials" that may or may not be well advertised. You can call around to find out if such special rates are offered and what they include. On weekends in some cities, rates are as little as one-half the usual charge, and the use of a pool or other athletic facility is often included at no extra fee. Other possible places to go are a retreat center, a church camp, a chapel, a backyard patio or gazebo. Whether the place is ordinary or unusual, it must be one that provides you with enough peace and privacy so that you feel personally ready to be alone with God.

And what if you feel a bit anxious or apprehensive? Consider that a hint that you're about to begin doing something significant.

Chapter 3

What You Need and What You Do

After you've decided where you're going to go to be alone
with God, you need to gather certain things and understand the plan presented in this book. A checklist will
help you get off to a good start. The list assures you of
having everything you need, and it can be used over and
over. If you decide to be in God's presence in this special
way on a regular basis you might store most of these items
in one container. I know a woman who schedules two
hours alone with God every other week and keeps her
"supplies" in a wicker basket. All she has to do is pick up
her basket and head for her favorite location, a bench in a
little park that is nearby, quiet, and safe.

Here are items you'll need along with this book:

_____ A Bible. Even though this book includes the
necessary scripture for each session, it's good to
have your own Bible. (When people ask me
which translation is best, I recommend they go
to a bookstore and read their favorite passages
from several translations and select the one
they favor. Some Bibles have study aids, cross-
references, even dictionaries of biblical terms in
the back or as footnotes.)

_____ Writing paper. Either a spiral-bound notepad or
a looseleaf binder with paper will be needed for
keeping notes.

_____ Two pens or pencils. You'll want two just in case
one breaks or goes dry while you're right in the
middle of writing.

_____ A timer or a clock that includes an alarm.

Here are nonessential items that many people have found to be useful in helping to create a comfortable and prayerful place:

_____   A cross or crucifix.

_____   A picture of Jesus or an icon. ("Icon" is the Greek word for "image" used in Genesis 1:26, which says that God created humans in his own "image." It has continued to be used in the Christian tradition of the East to refer to pictures of Jesus, his mother Mary, and holy men and women throughout Christian history. We can be encouraged on our spiritual path by following the examples of these faithful people of God.)

_____   A flower or flowers.

_____   A candle. A votive candle in a glass is least likely to cause an accidental fire in the event you should fall asleep with the candle burning.

_____   Incense.

_____   A cushion or blanket.

_____   A lightweight folding chair.

_____   Water or juice.

_____   Fruit or other light snack.

Set a Time

A minister with whom I'd been working complained that he was having trouble finding the time to sit quietly and pray. One Monday morning when we met, he showed me his appointment calendar. "Look here," he said, as he pointed to the filled page and began reading off what he had to do, hour by hour. Finally I broke in and asked, "What're you doing at eleven on Wednesday or Thursday?" "I'm busy Wednesday," he said, "but I've got the hour open on Thursday." "Put down prayer for that time slot," I suggested.

He was surprised by my suggestion but took it. After that I didn't see him for a couple of weeks, but the next time we met he told me he'd turned down a call for lunch at eleven on that particular Thursday and kept his time commitment to himself. Like so many other people I meet who are busy from morning till night, this minister was waiting to serve his own needs during what I call the "twenty-fifth hour"—the hour that never arrives.

What about you? Are you waiting for the twenty-fifth hour to give more attention to your spiritual life? If so, I suggest you make an appointment with yourself. Set a time to put aside all the clutter of your life and commit yourself to being alone with God.

If setting aside time for this purpose is a new experience for you, set a realistic and realizable goal. In the beginning, just taking the time is more important than the length of time. If you're using this book to take your "first" time alone with God, I recommend that you set aside at least one hour, but not more than two. On the other hand, if you are already disciplining yourself to pray, meditate, or read scripture on a schedule, you may be ready to set aside as much as four hours on a given day or plan an entire weekend.

Follow the Plan

The sessions outlined in Part Two of this book are all designed for a two-hour period and divided into a number of activities, each of which has a recommended time. If your schedule is very tight, it's important to use a timer so that you continue to move on and not stay overly long on any particular activity.

Which session should I do first? Although it's recommended that you do the sessions in sequence, each one is self-contained so you can rearrange the sequence to suit your personal needs and interests. For example, if you're troubled about forgiving or being forgiven, you may find help in the Seeking Forgiveness session and should begin there. Remember that being alone with God is meant to be an uplifting experience. Don't hesitate. Plunge into whatever topic is of most importance to you *at this time*. By doing so, you're likely to resolve the issue or at least get a new perspective on it.

What do I do if I have only one hour? Simply give each of the activities in the two-hour session you've selected one-half the listed time, or do half the session now and half later. Many of the suggestions can be picked up on at a later time. For example, you might find a few free minutes after your evening meal, during the time you'd normally watch TV, or just before bedtime.

Can anything go wrong? Not really. Of course you might be interrupted for some unforeseen reason. If that happens, you can always reschedule the time and begin again. It's not uncommon to fall asleep and then wake up and feel guilty when you discover how much time has slipped away.

Generally when I go to the Hermitage for a twenty-four-hour period, I go in the evening and stay until late the next afternoon. That allows for a good sleep and a fresh start in the morning. On one particular day, I began around 4:30 in the afternoon. My day had been hectic, so I lay down to rest a bit. I woke up at nine that evening, ate something, and then returned to my schedule. While reflecting on scripture, I fell asleep again and didn't wake up until the next morning! Earlier in my life as a spiritual director I would have felt terribly guilty, but now I was experienced enough to realize that God understands our needs better than we do. At that time my need was for sleep, and God provided it. I must admit, though, that I felt rather sheepish when I told my wife what had happened.

If you fall asleep while praying, consider it a clue to be followed up on. Are you working under too much pressure? Do you need to gentle the pace of your body and mind before going on? Remember that God is calling us to be whole persons and that it's okay to rest in God's presence as well as pray.

I might add that it's not unusual to cry during a session that has direct personal meaning. The tears may be the result of simply being unburdened or may be a part of the wonder and joy that come from being forgiven and accepted just as you are. (If this is your experience, you may find it helpful to read about the gift of tears in Chapter 9 of *The Breath of Life: Discovering Your Breath Prayer.*

The Plan

When people begin to purposely be alone with God, they prefer shorter periods of various activities rather than one lengthy reflection. So the plan I've developed divides the two hours into ten specific activities. The time allotted each is a guideline that you can change to suit your needs and desires. For example, if yours is a hectic life, you might double the time spent in silence and shorten the time spent on reading the scripture selection. Before making changes, go through at least one two-hour period just as it is outlined. Then if you feel the need, adapt the schedule.

This is what you'll be doing:

1. *Create an environment* (5 minutes). Get the space and yourself arranged so you'll be comfortable. Depending on where you are, this could include anything from unplugging the telephone at home to putting out a Do Not Disturb sign in a motel. You may want to arrange some flowers, light a candle, open your Bible, get comfortable on a cushion or in a chair.

2. *Open with brief prayer.* Begin with prayer to set the mood and theme for your time alone with God. A prayer is included with each section, and there are additional prayers in Part Three from which you may choose.

3. *Be still* (10 minutes). Do whatever helps you wind down from other activity and clear your mind. Some people find

that breathing deeply three or four times and relaxing the shoulders is a good way to get comfortable and be silent. Close your eyes and listen as you let yourself simply be with God. You may want to use a short prayer to bring your attention back into focus when you become aware that you're daydreaming or distracted—something like "Let me feel your presence, Lord" or "O God, lead me into peace." Coming back to repeat the Lord's Prayer or a favorite line from a hymn or psalm can serve the same purpose. Distractions are normal. Don't worry about them. Simply return to your short prayer and refocus your attention on the Lord.

4. *Read and reflect on scripture* (25 minutes). Each session includes the scripture to be read. You may read it from your own Bible if you prefer. I suggest that people read it aloud to themselves because there is a power in hearing the spoken word even when it is our own. You may feel embarrassed at first, but that feeling will disappear. As you read, let God's Spirit lead you. There is no need to "get through" the reading quickly. Let any personally meaningful word or line or image do what it will. It may trigger a prayer or a memory or another thought about God. Pray that prayer, pursue that memory or thought. If you feel the urge to write something down, do so.

Reread the same selection again and again, being ever aware that God is present. Perhaps the first or second reading doesn't strike a chord. But continue to reread the passage until the time is up, even if you feel you have tired of it and it is repetitious, because the reading will have an impact on you before your alone time is over.

Many people these days are expressing their concern about God being referred to with only masculine nouns and pronouns. Churches and church groups are suggesting a variety of solutions. Realizing that there is no universal solution at the moment and that the issue will be unresolved for some time, I've selected scripture from the RSV, a familiar and popular translation. During this transitional time, I use the word "God" in most of my writing, but I also use the masculine word "Lord" on occasion. I try to include as few masculine pronouns as possible but admit I'm a writer caught in the middle! God is love, and love is neither masculine nor feminine. It is both. I sincerely hope that both those of you who want to keep things just as they are and those of you who want sexist language changed as quickly as possible appreciate the writer's dilemma and will be understanding.

5. *Consider another dimension* (15 minutes). I've prepared a reflection to provide another dimension to the scripture reading. This is a brief meditation that presents another view of the passage or enables you to see an aspect of the story that you may not have considered before.

6. *Take a break to rest or walk* (15 minutes). We all need time for things to "settle in," so take a break. If possible, get outside and breathe deeply as you walk and stretch. Have some water or juice or a piece of fruit. If you feel drowsy, take a nap.

7. *Consider the inner dimension* (30 minutes). This period is devoted to inner reflection and (usually) a task designed to help you clarify God's action in your life. The inner dimension sections vary in content but generally require you to use your notebook. Depending on how freely you write, you may feel that too much or too little time has been allotted for this activity. Extend or shorten the time accordingly. If you finish quickly, go back over what you've written and allow God's Spirit to lead you to some other insight.

8. *Pray your response* (10 minutes). Pray in your own prayer style, or use a prayer from Part Three. The time may seem long if you are new to prayer or have never prayed for more than a few seconds at a time. Close your eyes to cut out distractions, and simply speak honestly to God about your feelings.

9. *Reflect* (10 minutes). This is a time to review what you have been doing while alone with God. People report

various experiences: a rediscovery of how to pray, an insight regarding scripture, a desire to change a particular behavior, an emotional awakening.

10. *Close with brief prayer.* Closing prayers that relate to the themes are included. You may, however, choose one from Part Three or use your own prayer.

Although a retreat of even so brief a time as two hours can serve several functions, the main purpose is to provide an opportunity to be more closely with God, the source of all love. Nervousness or anxiety that we feel during or after the session could be an indication that it is a new experience with which we are still becoming comfortable, or it could point out that our relationship needs more attention than we've been giving it.

Chapter 4

How to Recognize Spiritual Growth

"Where am I on the spiritual path?" people ask. "How do I know if I'm growing?" Spiritual growth may be much less visible than physical growth, but that doesn't make it any less real. If we're working and sharing with a group of caring people or someone such as a spiritual director, we may be able to get some indication as to whether we're making progress. Unfortunately, very few people have a spiritual guide or friend available to help them, so they must find some way to measure progress on their own. To this end, a journal is the most helpful tool available.

Using a Journal

Often people who come to my conferences or meet me at the Hermitage readily admit they're in a state of confusion, with everything rolling around in their heads. As soon as they've shared their ideas they say, "Just getting it out has cleared up so much." Keeping a journal can serve somewhat the same function. Getting the various ideas you have into a written form gives you a permanent record that not only helps you keep important moments alive but also gives you benchmarks against which to chart your spiritual development. Although it's obviously more subjective than a literal yardstick, a journal can serve as a measure of spiritual growth, and I urge everyone I meet to begin keeping one.

If you've tried keeping a journal but failed, try again. We'll look at five different ways to accumulate enough journal entries to give you the sort of information about yourself you need to recognize the spiritual changes that are taking place.

1. *Random Note-taking*. A doctor I know keeps a small notebook in his jacket pocket at all times. Whenever something happens that he believes is potentially important in his spiritual development, he makes a note of it. The results wouldn't make sense to anyone but the doctor. If you feel there is some special meaning to the new ideas, insights, and remembrances that can be generated by anything from the change of the seasons to a visit to the old hometown, consider keeping a journal of random notes. Date the entries and write down as much or as little as you feel is important. A filled notepad may include everything from sayings you want to remember to comments on a book you read.

2. *Dream Recording*. One of the most specific journals you can keep is a record of your dreams. In keeping notes about your dreams, you may want to set up a code that tells you whether the events recorded came from a day dream or a sleep dream. Both are important. Although we all dream several times every night, there are people who find it extremely difficult to recall their sleep dreams. If you're one of these, put a pencil and pad right beside your bed and try to capture a few of your dreams whenever you wake up right after having them or immediately upon awakening in the morning. Or use a tape recorder. One problem with tapes is that they're harder to review than notebooks are. With tapes, you have to listen to everything, and that takes more time than it does to skim notes.

Scripture is filled with dream events. Jacob's dream and Joseph's interpretation of dreams are examples from the Old Testament. Should we begin to read books on the subject and try to interpret our own dreams? I think it's more important to begin immediately to record both sleeping and waking dreams than to interpret them. You don't need any specialized knowledge of dreams to recog-

Thank You
Covenant Partner

This is a somewhat unusual tape that I have sent you. The Lord gave me a message to share with pastors and Christian leaders in a meeting following the Miracle Crusade in Manila. I spoke very frankly and honestly about the "calling" they have for ministry and the challenges that come with that calling. While the message was for leaders, I felt that it was a message to be shared with my Covenant Partners.

Every one of us as believers are challenged to *"...walk worthy of the vocation wherewith ye are called..."* (Ephesians 4:1) I want to hear the words, "Well, done!" by my wonderful Lord when I see Him face to face, don't you? Perhaps as you listen to this teaching you will be impressed to share it with your pastor as an encouragement, or with someone you know who is praying about a call to the ministry.

Please accept this tape with my deepest thanks for your partnership in ministry. Thank you for your love and your faithful support for the work of the Lord.

Everlastingly at it,

Benny Hinn

"I will praise thee, O Lord my God, with all my heart: and I will glorify thy name forevermore." Psalm 86:12

nize dream patterns. Recurring dreams have easy-to-
understand messages. For example, if you daydream con-
stantly about leaving a job, it may be that you're unhappy
in some aspect of your life and should try to identify that
unhappiness and consider making necessary changes. If
you're interested in dreams, by all means begin a dream
journal, or make notes about your dreams in a random
journal.

3. *Dialogue Journaling.* If you often find yourself thinking one thing and saying another, you would probably find
it interesting and useful to keep a journal in which you
describe the dialogue that goes on between your thinking
self and your feeling self. How does what you think differ
from what you feel? Do you think that God is a grand-
fatherly type in the sky but feel that God must be more
than that? Do you think you're quite intelligent about
religious matters but feel you're practicing your faith at
about the grade-school level? Do you think you should
leave your church but feel it's so much a part of your
heritage that you could never change?

Some people question where the dialogue comes from
and can argue at great length about the conscious and the
unconscious, good and evil, God and self. Frankly, that
seems to me to be a way to avoid using the gift. Dialoguing
is one of the means God has given us to help clarify who we
are spiritually and what we should be doing.

Besides dialoguing with ourselves, we can dialogue
with others, including people in scripture. What a script
we could write about a conversation we'd have with a loved
one who is now dead but to whom we left many things
unsaid! What a script we could write based on Luke 21 if
we imagined ourselves walking on the way to Emmaus
and suddenly had Jesus at our side!

Consider dialoguing as one more good way you can
commit thoughts to your journal.

4. *Reflecting.* Writing in a journal after reflecting on
your day or on any specific event is another way to use a

journal creatively as a means of evaluating changes taking place in your spiritual life. It's best to make an entry
each day at the close of the day. Recall and reflect on what
experiences the day has brought and the insights that flow
from them. This is very much like keeping a diary. The
main difference is that you look for those events that seem
to have spiritual significance. (For more about this type of
journal keeping, read Chapter 12, "A Journal for Reflection," in *The Breath of Life: Discovering Your Breath
Prayer.*)

5. *Outlining Discovery Tasks.* This form of journaling is
really like a school assignment, in that you go through a
particular activity in the hope of discovering all you can
about any subject that has a direct bearing on your spiritual life. For example, you might find yourself at an
impasse because you can't accept the traditional idea that
God is an old man on a throne in the sky. You could use a
journal to sum up everything you can recall about the way
you were taught this concept, how you presently feel about
it, and what you really believe about God.

When working on any discovery task, you look to the
past to help clarify the present and make living in the
future more satisfying. If there is a serious issue involved,
your journal may become quite detailed before you feel the
matter is satisfactorily resolved. Often in this form of
journal you get at the subject best by working back from
the present, rather like peeling an artichoke layer by
layer to reach the heart.

Throughout the sessions, there are opportunities for
you to use a journal in all five of the ways just mentioned.
Of course you don't have to limit your writing to those days
when you spend time alone with God. If you've never kept
a journal before, begin during one of the sessions and then
try to set aside five or ten minutes at the same time each
day to make an entry reflecting on the day. Most people
find that one approach suits them better than another, so
experiment as you go along, and don't give up too soon.

Generally six weeks is a good trial time. If you're serious about your spiritual development, your journal entries will probably reveal changes that indicate you're growing—growing more prayerful, more disciplined, more concerned not only about yourself but about others as well. You're likely to smile as you look back at your early journal entries and realize that although you still have shortcomings, you're a different person. Thanks be to God!

Part Two

Plans for Your Time
Alone with God

This portion of the book contains nine self-directed retreats in individual two-hour sessions which can be combined to create extended periods of four, six, eight, or more hours. Although the sessions are arranged and numbered for ease of use, they are self-contained and may be reorganized in any order you prefer.

SESSION FORMAT

Creating the Environment	5 minutes
Opening Prayer	
Silence	10 minutes
Reading and Reflecting on Scripture	25 minutes
Another Dimension	15 minutes
Break/Rest/Walk	15 minutes
Inner Dimension	30 minutes
Prayer of Response	10 minutes
Reflection on Alonetime	10 minutes
Closing Prayer	
TOTAL	2 hours

Session 1

Our Many Faces

(Luke 10:30-35)

Creating the Environment

(5 minutes)
Take a few minutes to create a comfortable environment for your time alone with God. What you do depends on whether you're indoors or out, at home or away. If you're inside, do whatever is necessary to avoid being interrupted by the telephone or the doorbell. Get comfortable within your space by turning away from anything distracting and by setting up whatever will help you get into a proper frame of mind. You may want to open your Bible and place it within easy reach next to some flowers or a candle.

Will a picture of Jesus, a cross, a crucifix, or an icon help make you more aware of God's presence? If there is something that will help you focus your attention, place that favored item near the Bible or wherever you can easily look at it without being distracted. Before going on, have at hand everything you may need, including your notebook and pens or pencils.

The objective is the same whether you are indoors or out—to be settled before going further.

Opening Prayer

I give you thanks, O God, my Creator. I believe that you

love me and call me by name. You know my face as well as
my innermost thoughts. May I become more aware of your
love today as we are alone together. May I feel your presence and move closer to seeing you face to face. I pray as
your child and in Jesus' name. Amen.

Silence

(10 minutes)
Set your timer.

The purpose of these ten minutes is to relax the body
and prepare the mind and heart to become more attentive
as you enter into a special time alone with God. Often
when we first sit down, our minds are cluttered and we
feel distracted. Don't fight your thoughts or focus long on
those that come to mind. Instead, breathe deeply and
evenly as you reflect on scripture. Use a short prayer or
this line (Psalm 139:23) as a touchstone, and come back to
it over and over as you remain silent:

SEARCH ME, O GOD, AND KNOW MY HEART!

As you spend this ten minutes, allow yourself to relax.
Breathe deeply or sigh, if you feel the need to loosen tense
muscles.

Reading and Reflecting on Scripture

(25 minutes)
Set your timer.

The story for this session is the story of the Good
Samaritan, found in Luke 10:30-35.

Read the story over and over. You may like to read it
quietly and then again out loud. There is great power in
the spoken word, even when it is your voice and you are
the audience. Think how you are in some way like each
one of the characters in the story. You have almost half
an hour, so there is no need to rush. When something
about the story strikes you, reflect on that idea. Be open

to the Word, and allow God's Spirit to lead your thoughts.

"A man was going down from Jerusalem to Jericho, and he fell among robbers, who stripped him and beat him, and departed, leaving him half dead. Now by chance a priest was going down that road; and when he saw him he passed by on the other side. So likewise a Levite, when he came to the place and saw him, passed by on the other side. But a Samaritan, as he journeyed, came to where he was; and when he saw him, he had compassion, and went to him and bound up his wounds, pouring on oil and wine; then he set him on his own beast and brought him to an inn, and took care of him. And the next day he took out two denarii and gave them to the innkeeper, saying, 'Take care of him; and whatever more you spend, I will repay you when I come back.'"

Another Dimension

(15 minutes)
Set your timer.

The purpose of this activity is to look at another dimension of the story. Scripture often presents us with stories that reveal the many facets, or faces, of ourselves.

How am I like the robbers? I rob not only myself but others as well when I say such things as "Oh, I can't do that," "You're not smart enough," or "I'm too old." Other remarks that indicate there is a robber within us include "It'll never work" and "You wouldn't want to disappoint *me,* would you?" On the other hand, the robber doesn't have to *say* anything. A young man who read this story said, "I remember a *look* that I got as a kid, and now I find myself giving others that same look. It says, 'Don't you dare!' I was robbed, and now I rob others."

How am I like the person beaten on? Perhaps, like Bill, an attorney in his late thirties, we remember times when we wanted to cry for help but just felt beaten down and didn't seem to have the energy. Maybe we're like Sandra, a busy forty-five-year-old mother of two who said, "You get angry when all you want is someone to be compassionate but no one seems to care about you."

How am I like the priest? The priest who passes by may be like that part of ourselves that utters truisms but says them glibly so as not to get involved. Thoughts such as, "Just pray about it and it'll go away," "Be of good cheer," or "Keep a stiff upper lip." We say such things not only to others but to ourselves as well. Remember the last time you put off something that needed doing by saying, "I'll do it tomorrow"? That's one way of reacting like the priest in the story.

How am I like the Levite? When we step aside from those who need our help and simply say, "It'll do them good to work it out themselves; they'll learn that way," we're acting like the Levite. We're cool and rational. There are times when that's fine, but such an attitude can be a mask that prevents us from acting with the compassion that's called for and that God expects of us.

How am I like the Samaritan? The Samaritan has become a romantic and heroic figure whom we often envision as *looking* for opportunities to dash over without hesitation to do a good deed. Rather than being a do-gooder, he might very well have been more like us—wanting to help but feeling hesitant or even fearful. Perhaps the Samaritan asked, "Should I stop, or shouldn't I?" As a traveler in those days, he surely knew of dangers along the road but chose to stop anyway.

Like the Samaritan, we sometimes take the risk and do what we hope others would do for us. There is, after all, a Good Samaritan side to our personality.

How am I like the innkeeper? A grandmother who read

this story said, "That's me. I'm the innkeeper. In my younger days, I took in stray cats and dogs and frogs and gerbils the kids brought home. As the children grew up, I took in stray boys and girls and friends and was never sure how many there'd be for breakfast. Now the kids have kids and I'm back into stray dogs, cats, toys, and grandchildren." A nurse reminded me of another face of the innkeeper. She explained, "I'm the innkeeper who says, 'You pay and I'll provide the room and the care.'" Indeed, there are various ways of being an innkeeper both at home and on the job.

How am I like the beast of burden? There are days when most of us drag along with bent back and shuffling feet. We don't actually complain, but people looking at us know how burdened we feel. If anyone asked, we'd probably say with a bit of sarcasm, "Oh, I feel fine, but don't worry about me. I'll feel worse tomorrow!"

Shirley is a volunteer church worker who explained why she saw herself so clearly as the beast of burden. "I just let people pile the jobs on me," she admitted. "I'll get them done somehow." Although Shirley wouldn't think of complaining, she'd be both happier and more successful if she took on only those jobs she knew she could handle.

Have you ever felt dumped on? overworked? Then you definitely know what it's like to be the burdened animal.

It's not uncommon for readers of the Samaritan story to say they feel like observers who don't identify with any of the characters, so the final face I'd like to mention is that of the onlooker. If you feel that reading the story is like watching a movie that doesn't involve you, or is like looking down at the earth from a cloud, you're reading the story as an observer. The beautiful thing about God's word is that we can choose to be more than observers by moving purposefully into every Bible story. This requires only that we put aside some of our self-protective attitudes and risk identifying with others. While doing so, we may feel some of our own past hurts, but we will understand ourselves more fully and then have an opportunity to change the way we act toward others as well as toward ourselves.

Break/Rest/Walk

(15 minutes)
If you're feeling tired and need to rest, set your timer before lying down. If you're going for a walk, keep track of the time with your watch.

The purpose of this activity is to refresh yourself. Have a snack if you like, but whatever you do, continue to reflect in an easy way about the story of the Samaritan and how it helps you see the many facets of your own personality.

Inner Dimension

(30 minutes)
Set your timer.

Get out your writing materials.

The purpose of this activity is to review what only you and God know about all the faces you wear during a typical week. This review will give you a better understanding of the need to accept the wonderfully complex person God created—you. Certainly there are sides of ourselves we don't much care about, but once we're aware of *all* our faces we can take steps to reveal more often the very best that is within us.

Write in your notebook or on a separate sheet of paper. Try to think of two to five examples for each of the faces. If you don't complete the activity within thirty minutes, finish it later. If you're done quickly, look more deeply at yourself and add examples you overlooked.

*   *   *

Example

I'm like the robbers . . .

1. when I tell myself, "You can't do that. It's too hard for you."
2. when I say to my daughter, "That's not something girls can do."
3. when I tell a coworker, "I didn't think you'd do it right."
4. when I do tasks for others that they could and should do for themselves.
5. when I fail to vote and then speak negatively about those elected.

* * *

These are the faces to think and write about:
I'm like the robbers when I. . . .
I'm like the person beaten on when I. . . .
I'm like the priest when I. . . .
I'm like the Levite when I. . . .
I'm like the Samaritan when I. . . .
I'm like the innkeeper when I. . . .
I'm like the beast of burden when I. . . .

Prayer of Response

(10 minutes)
Set your timer.

The purpose of this time is to free you of distractions and allow you to be more attentive to God moving quietly within your mind and heart. All you need do is sit still and return to this line (Psalm 139:1) whenever your attention wanders:

O LORD, THOU HAST SEARCHED ME
AND KNOWN ME.

Reflection on Alonetime

(10 minutes)
Set your timer.

Get out your writing materials.

Now reflect on what God is revealing to you about your many faces that reflect both weaknesses and strengths. What you write in your notebook or journal must be personal and honest. Among the key ideas you wrote down during the Inner Dimension activity, there is probably one that stands out. If so, give it more thought now. To get an idea of how others have approached this task, consider what a young single woman named Sandra wrote:

> The main insight for me this morning was that I tend to see myself as a beast of burden in my present job. I approach everything as if it is another instance of having something laid on me. I suspect that if I change my own attitude about myself I will be able to say no to some things that I realize I can't do. This will help me stop feeling so guilty when I don't get things done on time.

Tom, a graduate student, wrote from quite a different perspective:

> I never permit myself to think of any time when I've been the beaten-on one. The insight I had was that that may be the reason why I get so angry when I hear about anyone out of work or people on welfare. My own inability to see myself as one who needs help hinders me from seeing that anyone would ever need help. Yet, down deep, I truly know I've been beaten on. Maybe that's why my girlfriend says that I'm cold and never seem to need anything. That needs to change.

Now it's your turn to write. What is God helping you to see about yourself today? Which of your faces are you aware of in a new way? If there is something you would like to change about yourself, outline the steps that would help you change. Make them as practical as possible.

Closing Prayer

(If you prefer, use an alternate prayer or psalm from Part Three or pray the Lord's Prayer.)

O God, I give you thanks for this quiet time of reflection. I know that you love me and call me by name. You know me better than I know myself. May I come to a fuller understanding of who I am and do your will in the days ahead. I pray in Jesus' name. Amen.

Session 2

Seeking Forgiveness

(John 8:2-11)

And Jesus said,
"Neither do I condemn you;
go, and do not sin again."

Creating the Environment

(5 minutes)

Take a few minutes to create a comfortable environment
for your time alone with God. What you do depends on
whether you're indoors or out, at home or away. If you're
inside, do whatever is necessary to avoid being interrupted by the telephone or the doorbell. Get comfortable
within your space by turning away from anything distracting and by setting up whatever will help you get into
a proper frame of mind. You may want to open your Bible
and place it within easy reach next to some flowers or a
candle.

Will a picture of Jesus, a cross, a crucifix, or an icon help
make you more aware of God's presence? If so, place your
favored item near the Bible or wherever you can easily
look at it without being distracted. Have at hand everything you may need, including your notebook and pens or
pencils.

The objective is the same whether you are indoors or

43

out—to be settled before going further.

Opening Prayer

Almighty God, help me to become more attentive. Grant
me the wisdom to see myself clearly, recognize my faults,
and know when to turn to you for forgiveness. I come today
seeking the peace that can come only from you. Forgive
me and help me find the courage I need to forgive myself. I
pray in the name of Jesus. Amen.

Silence

(10 minutes)
Set your timer.

The purpose of these ten minutes is to relax the body
and prepare the mind and heart to become more attentive
as you enter into a special time alone with God. Often
when we first sit down, our minds are cluttered and we
feel distracted. Don't fight your thoughts or focus long on
those that come to mind. Instead, breathe deeply and
evenly as you reflect on scripture. Use this line (Psalm
55:1) as a touchstone, and come back to it over and over as
you remain silent:

GIVE EAR TO MY PRAYER, O GOD.

Reading and Reflecting on Scripture

(25 minutes)
Set your timer.

The story for this session is the story of the woman
caught in adultery, found in John 8:2-11.

Read the story at least three times.

First Reading: Imagine the story from the perspective
of Jesus. Attempt to sense his feelings and thoughts.

Second Reading: Imagine the story from the perspective of the Pharisees. Try to sense their feelings and

thoughts.

Third Reading: Imagine the story from the perspective of the woman. Try to sense her feelings and thoughts.

You may like to read the story quietly and then again out loud. There is great power in the spoken word, even when it is your voice and you are the audience. You have almost half an hour, so there is no need to rush. When something about the story strikes you, reflect on that idea. Be open to the Word, and allow God to lead your thoughts.

> Early in the morning he [Jesus] came again to the temple; all the people came to him, and he sat down and taught them. The scribes and the Pharisees brought a woman who had been caught in adultery, and placing her in the midst they said to him, "Teacher, this woman has been caught in the act of adultery. Now in the law Moses commanded us to stone such. What do you say about her?" This they said to test him, that they might have some charge to bring against him. Jesus bent down and wrote with his finger on the ground. And as they continued to ask him, he stood up and said to them, "Let him who is without sin among you be the first to throw a stone at her." And once more he bent down and wrote with his finger on the ground. But when they heard it, they went away, one by one, beginning with the eldest, and Jesus was left alone with the woman standing before him. Jesus looked up and said to her, "Woman, where are they? Has no one condemned you?" She said, "No one, Lord." And Jesus said, "Neither do I condemn you; go, and do not sin again."

Another Dimension

(15 minutes)
Set your timer.

The purpose of this activity is to look at another

dimension of the story. In this case, we'll consider four moods that are brought about by what people say or do.

There is a mood of *anticipation* in the crowd that has come to the temple to hear what Jesus will say. The anticipation grows, and we can imagine Jesus speaking.

There is a definite shift in the mood as the Scribes and Pharisees barge into the midst of the crowd. They have a victim to parade before the group. One can sense a tone of *hostility* as the Pharisees issue a bold and cunning challenge. They attempt to finally entrap Jesus by pitting him against the Law. In the face of such hostility, what can Jesus possibly do?

Jesus does not even deal with the question. He will not be tricked by hostility. Instead, he moves to the level of loving the woman *and* the Pharisees *and* the scribes. Rather than pit himself against the Old Law, he fulfills it with his love. The tone shifts to one of *silent tension* that remains until Jesus says, "Let him who is without sin among you be the first to throw a stone at her." It is a most unusual response. In dealing with hypocrisy, Jesus is answering falsehood that masquerades under the guise of keeping the Law. He condemns no one. Instead of arguing against the stoning, Jesus actually gives a suggestion on how it might take place!

At this point in the story, *tension increases*. As Jesus returns to writing on the ground, people slip away one by one until finally only Jesus and the woman remain. She has faced death at the hands of the crowd and now stands before an even more awesome power. Imagine how it feels to be in the presence of someone who faced down a hostile challenge.

Jesus looks up and asks, "Has no one condemned you?" and the woman says, "No one, Lord." The dramatic conclusion is brought about by Jesus' simple statement, "Neither do I condemn you; go, and do not sin again."

The tension is gone. Reading this scriptural passage helps us understand that sin is death and that sinning no more is life. Forgiveness separates the two.

This story is about my life and your life, and it raises questions we must face if we are to continue growing as Christians:

When do I place myself in a judging position?

When have I condemned someone else for an action I considered sinful?

When am I self-righteous in front of others?

When have I felt the Lord turning to me and saying that I am not condemned and that I should go and sin no more?

Break/Rest/Walk

(15 minutes)

If you're feeling tired and need to rest, set your timer before lying down. If you're going for a walk, keep track of the time with your watch.

The purpose of this activity is to refresh yourself. Have a snack if you like, but whatever you do, continue to reflect in an easy way about the story of the woman taken in adultery and your understanding of it.

Inner Dimension

(30 minutes)

Set your timer.

This activity focuses on a life review meant to help you discover specific ways in which you "miss the mark" and thus fail to live up to your potential.

"Sin" is a word that calls forth a variety of responses. More and more, people are disturbed by their inability to determine what is and what isn't sin. What one generation views as sinful, another may consider natural and normal. This is not only distressing to individuals but can actually split congregations into angry camps. One way to get some perspective on how viewpoints can change involves looking back to scripture. The word "sin" in

Greek is *hamartia,* which means "missing the mark."
Implied in this concept is the fact that there is a recogniz-
able "mark." That mark is the Christian's target. Inter-
estingly, "sin" is an old English archery term. When the
archer missed the mark, the judge called, "Sin."

What is the mark at which the Christian is aiming?
What is our call? How we answer depends, at least in part,
on our age. For example, a young child quickly learns that
we hope to one day be with God, so that becomes the
"mark" aimed for. Unfortunately, God may be viewed as a
giant police officer in the sky who watches over everything
and expects absolute obedience. This gives an unfortunate
connotation to sin, and the child finds it hard not to
confuse God's rules with Mom's and Dad's rules. Some
parents like it that way and use God to achieve good
discipline. When this is the case, God's love can seem
harsh or even nonexistent.

As we grow older and come to understand Jesus more
completely, we discover that God sent Jesus to be in our
midst, to walk with us and touch our lives. We are called to
have a living relationship with him. Many new ideas come
into focus then. Along with the childhood image and the
ten commandments, we are confronted with the loving
justice revealed through Jesus. What we saw as "sin" or
"missing the mark" must be more broadly defined. Many
people prefer the simple right/wrong, black/white, police-
officer image because it involves clear-cut rule following
that can be judged rather easily. On the other hand, the
addition of Jesus' loving justice often leads to dilemmas
that involve making personal moral decisions without the
help of a clearly defined law or rule.

The point I want to make clear is that although people's
understanding of sin may differ, every one of us can look
within and discover very specific ways in which we have
"missed the mark." Yes, all have sinned and fallen short of
the glory of God.

*   *   *

Get out your writing materials.

In the time that remains, do a *life review*. Write "Missing the Mark" at the top of a sheet of paper. Under that, make a list of ways in which you have not lived up to your potential as a child of God. Begin with the most recent time that you "missed the mark," and work back in time. Write down the date, event, or people involved. What you write is for *your* eyes only, but use abbreviations or fictional names if you would be embarrassed to have anyone else read the list in the event you lost it or someone picked it up by mistake.

There is no need to dwell on any of the events; just accept them as facts that are part of your spiritual history. If this exercise is painful, remember the woman in the story. Jesus did not demand that she become something she was not. He accepted her. The Lord does the same with us. Often we wish to hide our past rather than confront it; but remember that there is no time when God does not love us. There is no time, no matter what we have done, when Jesus is not willing to say, "Neither do I condemn you; go, and do not sin again."

Make your *life review* as complete as possible in the remaining time.

Prayer of Response

(10 minutes)
Set your timer.

This is a time to take responsibility for our sinfulness, seek forgiveness, and allow God to move quietly within your mind and heart.

Look over the list you made. It reflects a part of you, so acknowledge it, accept it. No matter how foolish or vile you perceive your actions to have been, embrace them now. Then place them at Jesus' feet just as the woman was placed before him. You can do this symbolically by placing your list in your Bible or on a table or an altar. You may burn the list as a symbol of accepting that part of yourself and receiving forgiveness.

Sit still and return to this phrase (Psalm 57:1) whenever your attentiveness wanders:

BE MERCIFUL TO ME, O GOD.

Reflection on Alonetime

(10 minutes)
Set your timer.

Get out your writing materials.

Now reflect on how loving and gracious God is to you and everyone else who returns to God in honesty and truth. Write down some of your feelings about "missing the mark" over the years. Is there any specific way in which you have fallen down again and again? If there is, write about why this has happened. You may find the key that will enable you to change.

Closing Prayer

(If you prefer, use an alternate prayer or psalm from Part Three, or pray the Lord's Prayer.)
O God, after looking at my life, I realize how often I miss the mark. I thank you for your loving gift of forgiveness and ask you to strengthen me. I pray for people everywhere who are mean-spirited and hold grudges. May they come to realize that your love and forgiveness, which Jesus made real in our world, are available to everyone. I pray in Jesus' name. Amen.

Session 3

Forgiving Others

(Matthew 18:23-35)

"And out of pity . . . the
Lord . . . forgave the debt."

Creating the Environment

(5 minutes)
Take a few minutes to create a comfortable environment for
your time alone with God. What you do depends on whether
you're indoors or out, at home or away. If you're inside, do
whatever is necessary to avoid being interrupted by the
telephone or the doorbell. Get comfortable within your space
by turning away from anything distracting and by setting
up whatever will help you get into a proper frame of mind.
You may want to open your Bible and place it within easy
reach next to some flowers or a candle.

Will a picture of Jesus, a cross, a crucifix, or an icon help
make you more aware of God's presence? If so, place your
favored item near the Bible or wherever you can easily look
at it without being distracted. Have everything at hand you
may need, including your notebook and pens or pencils.

The objective is the same whether you are indoors or
out—to be settled before going further.

Opening Prayer

O God, I know that you have forgiven me many times over.

Help me to sense your presence today so that I am encouraged and have the desire to forgive those people who I feel have offended me. Let me be loving toward them as you have taught me to be, and let me know that I will be forgiven just as I forgive. I pray in Jesus' name. Amen.

Silence

(10 minutes)
Set your timer.

The purpose of these ten minutes is to relax the body and prepare the mind and heart to become more attentive as you enter into a special time alone with God. Often when we first sit down, our minds are cluttered and we feel distracted. Don't fight your thoughts or focus long on those that come to mind. Instead, breathe deeply and evenly as you reflect on scripture. Use a short prayer of your own or this line (Psalm 42:2) as a touchstone, and come back to it over and over as you remain silent:

MY SOUL THIRSTS FOR GOD.

Reading and Reflecting on Scripture

(25 minutes)
Set your timer.

The story for this session is the story of the settlement of accounts, found in Matthew 18:23-35.

Read the story over and over. You may like to read it quietly and then again out loud. There is great power in the spoken word, even when it is your voice and you are the audience. Consider how the story applies to times when you have been in a position to be forgiving. Be open to the Word, and allow God to lead your thoughts.

"Therefore the kingdom of heaven may be compared to a king who wished to settle accounts with his servants. When he began the reckoning, one was brought to him who owed him ten thousand talents; and as he couldn't pay, his lord ordered him to be sold, with his wife and children and all that he had, and payment to be made. So the servant fell on his knees, imploring him, 'Lord, have patience with me, and I will pay you everything.' And out of pity for him the lord of that servant released him and forgave him the debt. But that same servant, as he went out, came upon one of his fellow servants who owed him a hundred denarii; and seizing him by the throat he said, 'Pay what you owe.' So his fellow servant fell down and besought him, 'Have patience with me, and I will pay you.' He refused and went and put him in prison till he should pay the debt. When his fellow servants saw what had taken place, they were greatly distressed, and they went and reported to their lord all that had taken place. Then his lord summoned him and said to him, 'You wicked servant! I forgave you all that debt because you besought me; and should not you have had mercy on your fellow servant, as I had mercy on you?' and in anger his lord delivered him to the jailers, till he should pay all his debt. So also my heavenly Father will do to every one of you, if you do not forgive your brother from your heart."

Another Dimension

(15 minutes)

Set your timer.

This time is an opportunity to look at another dimension of the story. In this case, we see an example of what happens when a person has sight but no vision insofar as forgiveness is concerned.

Anyone who has fallen behind on paying bills can certainly identify with the panic the servant feels when the king calls for an immediate settling of accounts. The servant, his wife and children, and their possessions are to be sold so that the debt can be repaid. There is no time to think, no time to borrow. The day of reckoning is at hand. In desperation, the servant falls to his knees and requests an extension of time, just as we would do if the bank called to foreclose on our car or home or farm or business.

The servant's desperate plea brings forth the kind of compassionate response that was as unusual in biblical times as in our own day. Occasionally (usually during the Christmas season) we read a newspaper story about someone forgiving or paying off the debt of another, but such events are so unusual that they make the news.

We can imagine how the servant feels upon hearing the king's response to his plea. The weight of ruin has been lifted from his shoulders. His debt is forgiven! He rises from his knees and goes his way. The sad story appears to have a happy ending and reminds us of an oldtime melodrama in which the heroine is saved from disaster in the nick of time. But in this case, the story is not yet over. As the servant goes about his business, he appears to have learned nothing from his own experience. All he can see is his own selfish interests. He has sight, but no vision. Self-interest overshadows him, and he refuses to do to others the kindness that has been done to him. When it comes to being forgiving, he has a very short memory.

What about us? Are we able to see the right thing done and pass along such kindness, or do we, like the servant, have sight but no vision? Think for a moment of all the times we've prayed the phrase "Forgive us our trespasses as we forgive those who trespass against us." We pray the words, but do we really mean them? *Do we truly want God to forgive us just as we forgive others?* If so, we may be wise to consider very carefully just how forgiving we are!

Mike was in jail serving time for a felony when he first heard this story that Jesus tells to answer Peter's question about how many times he must forgive another's sins. Mike found the story especially meaningful. He said, "I was struck that Jesus seemed to say so clearly to me that I've been forgiven more than I can ever forgive someone else. For a long time I didn't think I could ever be forgiven by God. But one day it connected. I made a list right then and there and started forgiving people."

Not all of us are quite so forthright. As Sandra, another person with whom I have worked, said, "When I owe something to someone I generally send it by mail. There's something about not wanting to see the person face to face when I'm in their debt. And then, I usually don't even like sending a letter with the payment. I try to make it as impersonal as possible. And I've noticed that the person to whom I'm in debt never mentions it either."

Truly, the servant in the story who is forgiven and then does not forgive his friend is a universal character with whom we can all identify in some way.

When it comes to forgiveness, are you shortsighted? Or do you have a clear vision of the need to both seek and grant forgiveness?

Have you ever been in Mike's position and realized that the story Jesus told applies directly to you and your life?

Are you at all like Sandra, who tries to avoid those to whom she is in debt?

Break/Rest/Walk

(15 minutes)
If you're feeling tired and need to rest, set your timer before lying down. If you're going for a walk, keep track of the time with your watch.

Refresh yourself. Have a snack if you like, but whatever you do, continue to reflect in an easy way about your attitude toward forgiving others.

Inner Dimension

(30 minutes)
Set your timer for fifteen minutes only.

Get out your writing materials.

The purpose of this activity is to review your life in a systematic way in order to recognize hurtful relationships that are still in need of healing—healing that can best come about through total forgiveness on your part.

1. At the top of a sheet of paper, write: "People who have hurt me, harmed me, or done something against me."

2. Pray the Lord's Prayer.

3. Spend fifteen minutes making a list of people who have hurt, harmed, or done something against you. Begin in the present and work back in time. There is no need to go over the events in detail; just write down a name or initials.

4. At the end of the time, reset the timer for another fifteen minutes and pray the Lord's Prayer again.

5. Spend the remainder of your time forgiving the people on your list, one by one. Imagine that the person is with you, and simply say, "_____(name)_____ I forgive you." Then, in your own words, pray for that person in a prayer such as this:

> God, you have forgiven me and love me as I am. Release any hurt or anger I have toward _____(name)_____ and bless our relationship. I seek only good for _____(name)_____. Transform our hearts so that we can forgive one another. I pray in Jesus' name. Amen.

6. Continue down your list. There may be some people you are not ready to forgive. That's all right. You can come back to this session another time and repeat it. Do what you can do now. Trust in the Lord. Even if you are able to forgive only one person in the allotted time, you've begun to live out the prayer that Jesus taught us to pray.

Prayer of Response

(10 minutes)
Set your timer.

The purpose of this activity is to free you of distractions

and allow God's presence to move quietly within your mind and heart. All you need do is sit still and return to this line (Psalm 66:19) whenever your attention wanders:
TRULY GOD HAS LISTENED.

Reflection on Alonetime

(10 minutes)
Set your timer.
Get out your writing materials.
Now reflect on what God is revealing to you about forgiveness. What you write in your notebook or journal should reveal your deepest response. If you feel tearful, allow yourself to cry. For an idea of how others have approached this task, consider the following journal entry by Joan, a widow in her sixties:

> After making my list of people who had done something against me, I was aware that I was relieved to have it out on paper. Even though some names were painful to remember, and I had forgiven them long ago, I discovered there was still hurt or some anger there.
>
> So I asked the Lord to release me from all that was holding me back. I found it interesting that some of the people had died already, and yet when I asked their forgiveness it was like they were right in front of me.
>
> I didn't make it through my list today, but I didn't feel like I had to either. I know that I've gotten names out into the open, and now I can be freer than ever before.

Now it's your turn to write. Was forgiving difficult? How did your feelings change as you went on? What prevented you from forgiving before?
Consider sending a note or letter to anyone from whom you have been cut off but whom you now feel able to

recontact in a spirit of love.

Closing Prayer

(If you prefer, use an alternate prayer or psalm from Part
Three, or pray the Lord's Prayer.)

O God, sometimes I forget I am under your protection and
that you love me beyond what I can imagine. Thank you
for forgiving all my trespasses through Jesus. Help me to
go on being released from all hurt and anger toward
others and to be ever mindful that it is up to me to be
forgiving. I ask this in Jesus' name. Amen.

Session 4

Receiving New Sight

(Luke 18:35-43)

[Jesus] asked him,
"What do you want me to do for you?"

Creating the Environment

(5 minutes)

Take a few minutes to create a comfortable environment for your time alone with God. What you do depends on whether you're indoors or out, at home or away. If you're inside, do whatever is necessary to avoid being interrupted by the telephone or the doorbell. Get comfortable within your space by turning away from anything distracting and by setting up whatever will help you get into a proper frame of mind. You may want to open your Bible and place it within easy reach next to some flowers or a candle.

Will a picture of Jesus, a cross, a crucifix, or an icon help make you more aware of God's presence? If so, place your favored item near the Bible or wherever you can easily look at it without being distracted. Have at hand everything you may need, including your notebook and pens or pencils.

The objective is the same whether you are indoors or out—to be settled before going further.

Opening Prayer

O God, I humbly place myself in your presence. At times

it's difficult for me to realize that I'm created in your image and likeness, because I know there are parts of my life that need to be healed. Help me today to be open to the love that Jesus makes real. Help me to see every day in a new light and make the best use of it. I pray in Jesus' name. Amen.

Silence

(10 minutes)
Set your timer.

The purpose of these ten minutes is to relax the body and prepare the mind and heart to become more attentive as you enter into a special time alone with God. Often when we first sit down, our minds are cluttered and we feel distracted. Don't fight your thoughts or focus long on those that come to mind. Instead, breathe deeply and evenly as you reflect on scripture. Use this line (Psalm 61:1) as a touchstone, and come back to read it over and over as you remain silent:

HEAR MY CRY, O GOD, LISTEN TO MY PRAYER.

Reading and Reflecting on Scripture

(25 minutes)
Set your timer.

The story for this session is the story about the blind man who was made to see; it is found in Luke 18:35-43.

Read the story over and over. You may like to read it quietly and then again out loud. There is great power in the spoken word, even when it is your voice and you are the audience. Try to enter the situation by imagining yourself at the city gate where beggars and merchants are clamoring for attention as people move along the dirt road. You have almost half an hour, so there is no need to rush. When something about the story strikes you, reflect on that idea. Be open to the Word, and allow God's Spirit to lead your thoughts.

As he [Jesus] drew near to Jericho, a blind man was
sitting by the roadside begging; and hearing a multi-
tude going by, he inquired what this meant. They
told him, "Jesus of Nazareth is passing by." And he
cried, "Jesus, Son of David, have mercy on me!" And
those who were in front rebuked him, telling him to
be silent; but he cried out all the more, "Son of David,
have mercy on me!" And Jesus stopped, and commanded him to be brought to him; and when he came
near, he asked him, "What do you want me to do for
you?" He said, "Lord, let me receive my sight." And
Jesus said to him, "Receive your sight; your faith has
made you well." And immediately he received his
sight and followed him, glorifying God; and all the
people, when they saw it, gave praise to God.

Another Dimension

(15 minutes)
Set your timer.

The purpose of this activity is to look at another dimension of the story and the special meaning it can have for us
as individuals.

Even those of us who can see, sometimes find ourselves
"in the dark" about some aspect of our life. Whenever
we're in need of healing but unsure how to proceed, the
story of the blind man is a reminder of how we must act.
Jesus did not seek out the blind man. Rather, the blind
man sought out Jesus, and that is exactly what we must
do. But there is more. Jesus demands that we speak for
ourselves and be specific concerning our need. Jesus asks
the blind man, "What do you want me to do for you?" The
man responds, "Lord, let me receive my sight."

These two important points—personally seeking out
Jesus and telling him our specific needs—are the keys to
receiving new sight. Nowhere in any of the miracles of

Jesus does the person who yearns for help respond, "Just do anything you'd like to do, Lord." The requests are always specific. This reminds us that we must take responsibility for our need and ask for the healing change. Do you generally seek out God? Can you be specific in your requests, or do you consider that selfish?

Often one of the difficulties is our inability to define exactly what's troubling us. When we're not well physically, we can check into the hospital and lie there day after day as other people test us until they find out what's wrong. It's not quite the same when we're not well spiritually. Even if we find someone who can help guide us, we still must do the work ourselves. The first step is believing—believing as the blind man did that Jesus has the power to heal whatever is wrong with us.

Break/Rest/Walk

(15 minutes)
If you're feeling tired and need to rest, set your timer before lying down. If you're going for a walk, keep track of the time with your watch.

This is a moment to refresh yourself. Have a snack if you like, but whatever you do, continue to reflect in an easy way about the story of the blind man and your understanding of it.

Inner Dimension

(20 minutes and then 10 minutes)
Set your timer for twenty minutes.

Get out your writing materials.

The purpose of this activity is to unveil something you're currently "in the dark" about but which is going to need healing somewhere along the spiritual path you're following.

Print the word "CRISES" at the top of a sheet of paper.

Then list all the big and little "crisis situations" that are, and have been, a part of your life. What is a crisis? It doesn't have to be a life-death situation, but it should be an event that makes your life run less smoothly than you'd like it to. A crisis may be a deadline missed at school or office, a forgotten appointment, a missed birthday, a guilty feeling about one of your personal relationships.

Begin with the most recent crisis and the approximate date it occurred (the other day, last week, last month, at Christmas).

* * *

Example

Yesterday.
  Disagreement with boss who never seems to listen to me.
  Late for dinner.
  Had a flat.
Last Friday.
  Lost temper, got mad at kids at breakfast, swore at them.
  Missed an important sale. Customer didn't seem to like me.
A week ago Friday.
  Felt frustrated all day.
  Drank too much before going home. Know it had something to do with the way I'm feeling at work.

* * *

Don't worry about remembering exact times and dates. As you work back in time, ask yourself, "When was the time before that?" and make a few notes about whatever crisis-type events come to mind.

Inner Dimension
(10 minutes)

Set your timer.

Look through your crisis list and see if you can discover any pattern. This is the entry a forty-year-old husband and father made in his journal after seeking patterns in his crisis list:

> The task wasn't as hard as I thought it would be. I didn't think I'd be able to recall many situations, but the Lord just seemed to be leading me to remember. One crisis memory triggered another. I was able to remember some things from childhood that I hadn't remembered in years. And I was amazed to see that a pattern was very clear to me. Many of the crisis situations I listed were times when I was feeling like I had to prove myself. This is what I can bring before God—my need to prove myself.

Beverly, a nurse who was single again as a result of a divorce, had quite a different experience when she did this activity. She wrote in her journal:

> After doing all this, some of which was painful, I became aware that I didn't *see* a pattern as much as *feel* one. I had the feeling of being a victim in situations and powerless to do anything. I immediately thought of one of my patients in intensive care who had told me he felt powerless and how at the time I had felt a strange identification with him. I know I'll be different when I see him again.

Look for a pattern in the entries on your crisis list. Perhaps it's similar to patterns that others have identified.

Do I always have to have my own way?
Is fear of failure holding me back?
Am I forever waiting for something to happen?

Do I look to others to save me and feel disappointed
    when no one does?
Do I create problems to get attention?

As clearly as possible, clarify your way of acting or
feeling, and write it down. Once you've recognized your
old way of responding, you're no longer in the dark about it
and can turn it over to the Lord.

Prayer of Response

(10 minutes)
Set your timer.

The purpose of this activity is to realize that Jesus is
waiting for us to call out to him and tell him what we want.

Look at the pattern you discovered. Up until now, it was
either something you chose not to recognize about yourself—something you have recognized but not yet dealt
with as openly as you could—or something you may have
been working on and now believe you have an opportunity
to finish. Like the blind man in the story, you were still in
the dark. But now, while sitting quietly, you can admit
your need to Jesus and receive new insights. Enter a
prayer dialogue with Jesus, speaking with him even more
intimately than you would with another friend. Come
back to this thought again and again:

(Jesus asks,)
"WHAT DO YOU WANT ME TO DO FOR YOU?"

"Lord, _____."
(Tell him what you want him to do for you.)

Reflection on Alonetime

(10 minutes)
Set your timer.

Get out your writing materials.

Now reflect on what you have discovered about yourself, and commit yourself to some new behavior patterns. It's important that you come out of the darkness willingly, remembering and believing that Jesus strengthens you when you do.

Be as objective about yourself as possible. Should you be paying more attention to others? taking better care of your health? praying or reading more? working on a personal relationship?

Closing Prayer

(If you prefer, use an alternate prayer or psalm from Part Three, or pray the Lord's Prayer.)

God, I know there are times when I'm in the dark about the way I act toward myself and others. Like the blind man, I know you're near, and I call to you now for your help. Although I'm weak sometimes, I do believe you hear all prayers. Today I pray especially that _____. Please help me to see anew and to be a light to others. I pray in Jesus' name. Amen.

Session 5

Calling to Jesus

(Matthew 14:22-33)

And Peter answered him,
"Lord, if it is you, bid me come to you on the water."

Creating the Environment

(5 minutes)
Take a few minutes to create a comfortable environment for your time alone with God. What you do depends on whether you're indoors or out, at home or away. If you're inside, do whatever is necessary to avoid being interrupted by the telephone or the doorbell. Get comfortable within your space by turning away from anything distracting and by setting up whatever will help you get into a proper frame of mind. You may want to open your Bible and place it within easy reach next to some flowers or a candle.

Will a picture of Jesus, a cross, a crucifix, or an icon help make you more aware of God's presence? If so, place your favored item near the Bible or wherever you can easily look at it without being distracted. Have at hand everything you may need, including your notebook and pens or pencils.

The objective is the same whether you are indoors or out—to be settled before going further.

Opening Prayer

Almighty God, I feel a great need that only you can

answer. I don't like to give up control, and at times I try to
go it alone. Give me the patience to be more attentive to
the presence of Jesus in my life. Help me to trust enough
so that I can admit my needs to Jesus, give my power over
to him, and listen for his response. I pray in Jesus' name.
Amen.

Silence

(10 minutes)
Set your timer.

The purpose of these ten minutes is to relax the body
and prepare the mind and heart to become more attentive
as you enter into a special time alone with God. Often
when we first sit down, our minds are cluttered and we
feel distracted. Don't fight your thoughts or focus long on
those that come to mind. Instead, breathe deeply and
evenly as you reflect on scripture. Use this line (Psalm
54:1) as a touchstone, and come back to it over and over as
you remain silent:

SAVE ME, O GOD, BY THY NAME.

Reading and Reflecting on Scripture

(25 minutes)
Set your timer.

The story for this session is the story about Jesus walking on the water; it is found in Matthew 14:22-33.

Read the story over and over. You may like to read it
quietly and then again out loud. There is great power in
the spoken word, even when it is your voice and you are
the audience. Think how you are in some way like the
characters in the story. You have nearly half an hour, so
there is no need to rush. When something about the story
strikes you, reflect on that idea. Be open to the Word, and
allow God to lead your thoughts.

Then he [Jesus] made the disciples get into the boat

and go before him to the other side, while he dismissed the crowds. And after he had dismissed the crowds, he went up on the mountain by himself to pray. When evening came, he was there alone, but the boat by this time was many furlongs distant from the land, beaten by the waves; for the wind was against them. And in the fourth watch of the night he came to them, walking on the sea. But when the disciples saw him walking on the sea, they were terrified, saying, "It is a ghost!" And they cried out for fear. But immediately he spoke to them, saying, "Take heart, it is I; have no fear." And Peter answered him, "Lord, if it is you, bid me come to you on the water." He said, "Come." So Peter got out of the boat and walked on the water and came to Jesus; but when he saw the wind, he was afraid, and beginning to sink he cried out, "Lord, save me." Jesus immediately reached out his hand and caught him, saying to him, "O man of little faith, why did you doubt?" And when they got into the boat, the wind ceased. And those in the boat worshiped him, saying, "Truly you are the Son of God."

Another Dimension

(15 minutes)
Set your timer.

The purpose of this activity is to look at another dimension of the story and what special meaning it can have for us as individuals. In this particular story, we'll examine three ideas in detail.

First, let's consider the placement of this story. It follows immediately after the feeding of 5,000 people with five loaves and three fish. The disciples are in the midst of this crowd and observe firsthand that after people have eaten their fill, there are plenty of leftovers. Within a few hours, however, the disciples face a problem that doesn't seem any more demanding than the feeding of the hungry, yet they appear to have totally forgotten Jesus' care and concern!

We're that way ourselves, quickly forgetful of past blessings.

A second dimension to consider about this story is the role of the wind. Although storms come up quickly on the Lake of Gennesaret, it's the wind's possible *direction* and not its stormy force that we'll consider. The boat is heading into the wind. Jesus, walking toward the boat, is walking into the wind. When Peter gets out of the boat to go toward Jesus, he has the wind at his back.

Let's think about the difference between a head wind and a tail wind. We've all struggled against a head wind and understand what great effort it takes to walk into one. But now think about the wind that comes from behind, the wind that might be rushing Peter faster than he wanted to go. Perhaps Peter felt himself losing control over the situation and wasn't quite ready.

We can be that way ourselves, pushed by the Spirit so rapidly toward God's wondrous love that we're not quite prepared.

The third dimension to ponder about this story is the call to have faith and move beyond whatever appears to be a secure position; to believe that there's power offered that we haven't yet experienced. Certainly the boat in the story doesn't seem to be a very comfortable refuge in a storm. It does, however, remind us that nothing earthly offers the security that Jesus offers. And yet, sometimes a rocking boat is better than nothing!

Break/Rest/Walk

(15 minutes)
If you're feeling tired and need to rest, set your timer before lying down. If you're going for a walk, keep track of the time with your watch.

Refresh yourself. Have a snack if you like, but whatever you do, continue to reflect in an easy way about the story of Peter and Jesus meeting on the water.

Inner Dimension

(30 minutes)

Set your timer.

Get out your writing materials.

The purpose of this activity is to look within your own life and see how the Lord is calling you and from what security the Lord is asking you to step out in faith in order to experience a new blessing.

Divide your paper into three sections, and give the sections these headings:

1	2	3
My blessings	My boat	Times I've felt the Spirit moving me faster than I would like to go toward Jesus

Under each of these, make specific notes that help describe your spiritual journey thus far in life.

* * *

Column 1: In what physical, mental, spiritual, and emotional ways do I feel God has gifted me?

Column 2: What gives me a sense of security and would be difficult to let go of?

Column 3: When have I felt the Spirit moving me faster than I'd like to go toward Jesus? In this column, reflect on those times when you felt that God was dealing with you a little too fast. Some people find this the most difficult question, so consider such things as prayer experiences, death of a loved one and your response to it, the call of an evangelist, your reaction to an inspiring book or movie. Think of a time when you said, "Yes, Lord, but not right now, please."

Prayer of Response

(10 minutes)
Set your timer.

The purpose of this activity is to become more attentive to thanking God for your blessings.

Look over your list of blessings. Although these have been a part of your life, what's already happened to you is only a taste of what is yet to come.

Sit still and return to this line (Psalm 57:7) whenever your attention wanders:

MY HEART IS STEADFAST, O GOD.

Reflection on Alonetime

(10 minutes)
Set your timer.

Get out your writing materials.

Now reflect on the reading and what it reveals about your spiritual life. This is what Jerry, a young computer programmer, wrote in his journal:

> I find that I can really identify with Peter calling to Jesus, and so I thought of the times that I've called out to Jesus to have me come to him. Then I was aware that I've always had problems stepping out of the boat. So I decided that maybe this scripture was calling me to look at what I really consider security for myself and what I refuse to get out of or let go of.

An elderly woman named Ruth wrote this reflection:

> I was struck by the fact that the disciples had just seen a miracle of feeding more than 5,000 people and

yet how easily they were distracted from what they had just experienced and got caught up in a new problem. That is so much like my life, it seems. If I really hear myself talk when I say, "Oh, I wish the Lord would be active in my life," I'd remember the many times the Lord has simply overwhelmed me with goodness. Maybe I don't rejoice in those events enough.

To what in your life right now is Jesus calling you? From what security is he asking you to step out in faith to experience a new blessing?

Closing Prayer

(If you prefer, use an alternate prayer or psalm from Part Three, or pray the Lord's Prayer.)

O God, you have called me time and time again to come toward you. Often I've refused to step away from my security. For these times, I'm sorry and seek forgiveness. At other times, I've stepped forward in faith and realized many blessings, for which I now give thanks. Let me feel the presence of your love and not be afraid of moving too fast into a deep and everlasting faith. Continue to fill me with your powerful Spirit. I ask this in Jesus' name. Amen.

Session 6

Freedom

(John 11:1-44)

Jesus said to them,
"Unbind him, and let him go."

Creating the Environment

(5 minutes)

Take a few minutes to create a comfortable environment for your time alone with God. What you do depends on whether you're indoors or out, at home or away. If you're inside, do whatever is necessary to avoid being interrupted by the telephone or the doorbell. Get comfortable within your space by turning away from anything distracting and by setting up whatever will help you get into a proper frame of mind. You may want to open your Bible and place it within easy reach next to some flowers or a candle.

Will a picture of Jesus, a cross, a crucifix, or an icon help make you more aware of God's presence? If so, place your favored item near the Bible or wherever you can easily look at it without being distracted. Have at hand everything you may need, including your notebook and pens or pencils.

The objective is the same whether you are indoors or out—to be settled before going further.

Opening Prayer

God, source of freeing love, I give you thanks for all the

wonders you place before me. At times I become self-centered and bound up by my own small world. In seeing my own needs so clearly, I forget the needs of others. Today, as I place myself in your presence, help me to understand and accept the freeing power of love that Jesus offers. I pray in Jesus' name. Amen.

Silence

(10 minutes)
Set your timer.

The purpose of these ten minutes is to relax the body and prepare the mind and heart to become more attentive as you enter into a special time alone with God. Often when we first sit down our minds are cluttered and we feel distracted. Don't fight your thoughts or focus long on those that come to mind. Instead, breathe deeply and evenly as you reflect on scripture. Use this line (Psalm 29:4) as a touchstone, and come back to it over and over as you remain silent:

THE VOICE OF THE LORD IS POWERFUL,
THE VOICE OF THE LORD IS FULL OF MAJESTY.

Read and Reflect on Scripture

(25 minutes)
Set your timer.

The story for this session is the story of Lazarus being raised from the dead; it is found in John 11:1-44.

Read slowly through the story at least twice. You may like to read it silently the first time and then out loud. There is great power in the spoken word, even when it is your voice and you are the audience. You have almost half an hour, so there is no need to rush. When something about the story strikes you, reflect on that idea. Be open to the Word, and allow God to lead your thoughts.

Now a certain man was ill, Lazarus of Bethany, the

village of Mary and her sister Martha. It was Mary who anointed the Lord with ointment and wiped his feet with her hair, whose brother Lazarus was ill. So the sisters sent to him, saying, "Lord, he whom you love is ill." But when Jesus heard it he said, "This illness is not unto death; it is for the glory of God, so that the Son of God may be glorified by means of it."

Now Jesus loved Martha and her sister and Lazarus. So when he heard that he was ill, he stayed two days longer in the place where he was. Then after this he said to the disciples, "Let us go into Judea again." The disciples said to him, "Rabbi, the Jews were but now seeking to stone you, and are you going there again?" Jesus answered, "Are there not twelve hours in the day? If any one walks in the day, he does not stumble, because he sees the light of this world. But if any one walks in the night, he stumbles, because the light is not in him." Thus he spoke, and then he said to them, "Our friend Lazarus has fallen asleep, but I go to awake him out of sleep." The disciples said to him, "Lord, if he has fallen asleep, he will recover." Now Jesus had spoken of his death, but they thought that he meant taking rest in sleep. Then Jesus told them plainly, "Lazarus is dead; and for your sake I am glad that I was not there, so that you may believe. But let us go to him." Thomas, called the Twin, said to his fellow disciples, "Let us also go, that we may die with him."

Now when Jesus came, he found that Lazarus had already been in the tomb four days. Bethany was near Jerusalem, about two miles off, and many of the Jews had come to Martha and Mary to console them concerning their brother. When Martha heard that Jesus was coming, she went and met him, while Mary sat in the house. Martha said to Jesus, "Lord, if you had been here, my brother would not have died. And even now I know that whatever you ask from

God, God will give you." Jesus said to her, "Your
brother will rise again." Martha said to him, "I know
that he will rise again in the resurrection at the last
day." Jesus said to her, "I am the resurrection and the
life; he who believes in me, though he die, yet shall he
live, and whoever lives and believes in me shall never
die. Do you believe this?" She said to him, "Yes, Lord;
I believe that you are the Christ, the Son of God, he
who is coming into the world."

When she had said this, she went and called her
sister Mary, saying quietly, "The Teacher is here and
is calling for you." And when she heard it, she rose
quickly and went to him. Now Jesus had not yet come
to the village, but was still in the place where Martha
had met him. When the Jews who were with her in
the house, consoling her, saw Mary rise quickly and
go out, they followed her, supposing that she was
going to the tomb to weep there. Then Mary, when
she came where Jesus was and saw him, fell at his
feet, saying to him, "Lord, if you had been here, my
brother would not have died." When Jesus saw her
weeping, and the Jews who came with her also weeping, he was deeply moved in spirit and troubled; and
he said, "Where have you laid him?" They said to
him, "Lord, come and see." Jesus wept. So the Jews
said, "See how he loved him!" But some of them said,
"Could not he who opened the eyes of the blind man
have kept this man from dying?"

Then Jesus, deeply moved again, came to the
tomb; it was a cave, and a stone lay upon it. Jesus
said, "Take away the stone." Martha, the sister of the
dead man, said to him, "Lord, by this time there will
be an odor, for he has been dead four days." Jesus said
to her, "Did I not tell you that if you would believe you
would see the glory of God?" So they took away the
stone. And Jesus lifted up his eyes and said, "Father, I
thank thee that thou hast heard me. I knew that thou

hearest me always, but I have said this on account of the people standing by, that they may believe that thou didst send me." When he had said this, he cried with a loud voice, "Lazarus, come out." The dead man came out, his hands and feet bound with bandages, and his face wrapped with a cloth. Jesus said to them, "Unbind him, and let him go."

Another Dimension

(15 minutes)
Set your timer.

Now let's look at another dimension of the story in order to discover personal meanings it may have for us.

Another way to study this story is by considering it as a play of six scenes. The scenes have characters and actions with which we may identify or through which we may gain insights for spiritual growth.

Scene 1: Jesus and his disciples receive the message about Lazarus, and there is misunderstanding. Jesus has an understanding and a plan that the others do not share. They are confused, but already we see Jesus taking the action forward. There is even a touch of humor in this scene as Jesus' words fly over the heads of his followers. The disciples don't see what Jesus is getting at when he talks about walking in the daylight because people can see the light of the world.

Scene 2: Jesus and his friends arrive at Bethany, where many Jews have come from Jerusalem to share in the grieving. Someone tells Martha that Jesus has arrived, and we have dialogue between Martha and Jesus that is theological in tone.

Scene 3: Martha returns to the house where Mary and the other women are grieving; perhaps they're sitting and talking softly as we might be in a funeral home or at the home of the deceased. Martha whispers to Mary, who then bolts out of the house. Mary goes to Jesus and blurts out

what is on her mind. The tone of the conversation is quite
different. Where Martha's theological talk might be sym-
bolic of the rational aspect of ourselves, Mary's words
might be the intuitive or emotive aspect. Notice, though,
that now both women are present with Jesus as the move-
ment of the drama continues.

Scene 4: This is a short but pivotal scene where Jesus
stands at the center of the stage. Jesus says, "Where have
you laid him?" and "Roll away the stone." Martha's blunt
words emphasize what she sees as the awful reality:
"There will be an odor."

Scene 5: There is a dramatic moving of the stone. The
end is swiftly approaching, and Jesus places himself in
the power of the Father and in the midst of the people. He
makes it clear what he is about.

Scene 6: Even Jesus is in the shadows as the last scene
opens with everyone looking to the tomb. One can feel the
tension as Jesus calls, "Lazarus, come out." Into the blaz-
ing light comes the man Lazarus, wrapped and bound.
After that peak dramatic moment, Jesus concludes wth
the final, freeing words: "Unbind him, and let him go."

Break/Rest/Walk

(10 minutes)
If you're feeling tired and need to rest, set your timer
before lying down. If you're going for a walk, keep track of
the time with your watch.

The purpose of this activity is to refresh yourself. Have
a snack if you like, but whatever you do, continue to reflect
in an easy way about the story of Lazarus.

Inner Dimension

(30 minutes)
Set your timer.
Now you have the opportunity to discover how some or

all of the Lazarus story relates to your journey with the Lord.

At some time in life, each of us experiences the scenes we outlined while thinking of the story as a dramatic play. Recall, if you can, a time of misunderstanding and confusion when you simply were unable to see what plan God intended for you. This was probably a time when you didn't understand the signs and had to plod along in a trusting way.

Now think of another instance when you were confronted by important words or actions that you felt were from God, or someone else you trusted, and tried to figure it out in your head. You pretty much ignored your feelings. Maybe you got into some theological talk, the way Martha did. There's nothing wrong with this approach, but we should be aware that it's a rather analytical approach that might ignore the "heart" of the question.

Recall, if you can, a time when, like Mary, you rushed to Jesus with your hurt and realized he not only knew what you were feeling but shared your pain.

Think back to an event that you kept buried like Lazarus behind the stone and weren't sure you wanted revealed. Did you eventually "take away the stone" and confront the issue, or are you still keeping it buried?

There was a time when you sensed Jesus moving closer and closer to you. How did you respond?

Recall, if you can, a time when you felt the power of God close at hand, had a deep sense of expectation, and then enjoyed a wondrous sense of release.

Each of us is Lazarus, and as we recall the details of the story, we can realize anew that we have been set free by the powerful words of Jesus.

Prayer of Response

(10 minutes)
Set your timer.

The purpose of this activity is to free yourself of distractions and allow God's Word to move quietly within your mind and body. All you need to do is sit still and return to this line (Psalm 51:10) whenever your attention wanders:
CREATE IN ME A CLEAN HEART, O GOD.

Reflection and Alonetime

(10 minutes)
Set your timer.
Get out your writing materials.
Now as you write, recognize that God calls you forth to freedom. Make a note of some personal insight or rediscovery that has come from your work with the story of Lazarus.

Closing Prayer

(If you prefer, use an alternate prayer or psalm from Part Three, or pray the Lord's Prayer.)
God, I thank you for sending Jesus to be the light of the world. Help me see that I am free from sin, darkness, and misunderstandings. Like Lazarus, I hear Jesus call me into the light. Encourage me to answer, and continue to fill me with love so that I might be like a light in the lives of people I know. I ask this in Jesus' name. Amen.

Session 7

Overcoming Anxiety

(Matthew 6:25-34)

"Therefore do not be anxious about tomorrow. . . ."

Creating the Environment

(5 minutes)
Take a few minutes to create a comfortable environment for your time alone with God. What you do depends on whether you're indoors or out, at home or away. If you're inside, do whatever is necessary to avoid being interrupted by the telephone or the doorbell. Get comfortable within your space by turning away from anything distracting and by setting up whatever will help you get into a proper frame of mind. You may want to open your Bible and place it within easy reach next to some flowers or a candle.

Will a picture of Jesus, a cross, a crucifix, or an icon help make you more aware of God's presence? If so, place your favored item near the Bible or wherever you can easily look at it without being distracted. Have at hand everything you may need, including your notebook and pens or pencils.

The objective is the same whether you are indoors or out—to be settled before going further.

Opening Prayer

O God of all creation, I want to believe that you care for us

always, but at times I feel anxious about what I have and
what I want to have. Help me to overcome my worries and
to realize that your loving care is ever present in my life.
Although I get distracted, I truly want to seek your kingdom first and to believe that all else will come to me as I
need it. I pray in Jesus' name. Amen.

Silence

(10 minutes)
Set your timer.

The purpose of these ten minutes is to relax the body
and prepare the mind and heart to become more attentive
as you enter into a special time alone with God. Often
when we first sit down, our minds are cluttered and we
feel distracted. Don't fight your thoughts or focus long on
those that come to mind. Instead, breathe deeply and
evenly as you reflect on scripture. Use a short prayer or
this line (Psalm 46:1) as a touchstone, and come back to it
over and over as you remain silent:

GOD IS OUR REFUGE AND STRENGTH.

Reading and Reflecting on Scripture

(25 minutes)
The story for this session is the story about the birds of the
air and the flowers of the field; it is found in Matthew
6:25-34.

Read the story over and over. You may like to read it
quietly and then again out loud. There is great power in
the spoken word, even when it is your voice and you are
the audience. Think how the story applies to your life at
this time. You have almost half an hour, so there is no need
to rush. When something about the story strikes you,
reflect on that idea. Be open to the Word, and allow God's
Spirit to lead your thoughts.

"Therefore I tell you, do not be anxious about your

life, what you shall eat or what you shall drink, nor about your body, what you shall put on. Is not life more than food, and the body more than clothing? Look at the birds of the air: they neither sow nor reap nor gather into barns, and yet your heavenly Father feeds them. Are you not of more value than they? And which of you by being anxious can add one cubit to his span of life? And why are you anxious about clothing? Consider the lilies of the field, how they grow; they neither toil nor spin; yet I tell you, even Solomon in all his glory was not arrayed like one of these. But if God so clothes the grass of the field, which today is alive and tomorrow is thrown into the oven, will he not much more clothe you, O men of little faith? Therefore do not be anxious, saying, 'What shall we drink?' or 'What shall we wear?' For the Gentiles seek all these things; and your heavenly Father knows that you need them all. But seek first his kingdom and his righteousness, and all these things shall be yours as well.

"Therefore do not be anxious about tomorrow, for tomorrow will be anxious for itself. Let the day's own trouble be sufficient for the day."

Another Dimension

(15 minutes)

Set your timer.

This section of Matthew's Gospel is part of a large discourse, or teaching, that Jesus gives, beginning with the beatitudes in Chapter 5. The teaching on the mount continues as Jesus talks about the everyday living out of the Spirit. In the passage we're considering, Jesus is talking to his followers about detachment from things.

Some people find this story threatening, but I think of Jesus' words here as a friendly and loving caution. In our own day, when someone is overly worried about something, we're likely to comment, "Oh, just relax and it'll take care of itself." We don't mean the person should do nothing; we do mean the person should put things in their proper perspective. I believe that Jesus was speaking in both a chiding and a loving way at this point in Matthew's Gospel.

I especially like verse 34, where Jesus reminds us that we should not be anxious about tomorrow. "Let the day's own trouble be sufficient for the day." Does this mean we're to ignore the future? Of course not. We're expected to deal creatively with our life and our needs, but there are times when we get so wrapped up in personal concerns that we lose sight of what's truly important and need to be reminded to pay attention to the problem or situation at hand. While Jesus is telling us to live in the *now,* this doesn't mean we're to live only for today or in a hedonistic lifestyle. He calls for balance; he tells us to focus our attention on what is important.

I think, for example, of two office workers who returned from vacation to find their desks piled high with work. One bemoaned the work ahead and frittered time away, feeling more anxious with every hour. The other set to work immediately, dividing the work into three piles according to importance. While the first worker was still complaining and growing ever more anxious, the second had her priorities in order and was getting on with the job in an ordinary but effective way.

Now imagine yourself in the crowd of people who are looking up to where Jesus is standing a little above them on the hillside. As he speaks, he makes use of what's around—birds flitting across the sky, flowers blossoming from the earth. He begins with a simple statement, "Do not be anxious. . . ."

People who begin to actively seek a deeper walk with God are often anxious about what's going to happen tomorrow, next week, next month. They can't decide whether to pray or read scripture, get involved in good works, or go off alone to meditate. They're anxious to *get some place* soon! Often they find it helpful to realize there's not necessarily a place to get to, but there is a life to live in a purposeful way.

Break/Rest/Walk

(15 minutes)
If you're feeling tired and need to rest, set your timer before lying down. If you're going for a walk, keep track of the time with your watch.

The purpose of this activity is to refresh yourself. Have a snack if you like, but whatever you do, continue to reflect in an easy way on what Jesus said.

Inner Dimension

(30 minutes)
Set your timer.

Get out your writing materials.

Devote this time to looking through your life to better understand what you may be anxious about. Also consider what steps to take to become more comfortable with your life.

Eating, drinking, the body, clothing, and tomorrow are five specific concerns Jesus mentioned. So, to begin this activity, divide a sheet of paper into five columns:

Eating   Drinking   Body   Clothing   Tomorrow

About which of these five do you worry the most? Print "1" over it.

About which of these five do you worry the least? Print "5" over it.

Now consider how anxious you are about the three remaining topics and rank then "2," "3," and "4."

Fill the column under your #1 selection with personal thoughts about the topic. Make your writing as specific as possible.

When did you first begin to be anxious?
Can you name the anxiety?
What is it doing to your life physically? mentally?
Is the problem more imagined than real?
How have you tried to avoid the issue? resolve it?

It's important to learn as much as you can about whatever is causing you to feel anxious. Making specific notes will help you decide whether you're ready to take the actions needed to lower your level of anxiety and possibly remedy the situation.

You can fill in all five columns if you like, but you may find it's more helpful to limit your focus today to only one or two areas of concern. You can continue the exercise at some future time.

Many people think that money is the answer to all problems. Of course an adequate income is important, but above a certain point more money really won't help. In fact, money can lead us to become accumulators who never seem to have enough possessions. Most of us are accumulators to some extent. We've got more shoes under the bed than we'll ever need, or a closet full of clothes we don't wear, or a special drawer full of private possessions we think we can't live without. We have compulsions to collect, store away, hide. One woman was so in love with her possessions that she was actually buried in her favorite car!

Jesus makes it clear that those who attempt to walk in the spirit of the kingdom don't seek an abundance of material things as their goal. Often we need to be reminded that we are created in the image of God and are called to be sojourners. We have another home and are here only on a journey, so we need only enough for our journey. Life isn't a collection station; it's a time for living fully but simply. Anxieties and concerns won't leave us, but we must handle them as best we can and get on with life as Jesus would have us live it. Simply.

Prayer of Response
(10 minutes)
Set your timer.

The purpose of this activity is to free you of distraction and allow God to move quietly within your mind and heart. All you need do is sit still and begin to see yourself as a person becoming free by relying upon the Lord more and more each day. Return to this line (Psalm 146:9) as you sit in silence:

THE LORD WATCHES OVER THE SOJOURNERS.

Reflection on Alonetime

(15 minutes)
Set your timer.

Get out your writing materials.

Now reflect on what God is revealing to you about those things that make you feel anxious. Look again at the thoughts you wrote out during the Inner Dimension activity. Begin planning some simple changes in your life—changes to help you overcome being anxious and to become more aware of being a sojourner, a traveler passing through this life. To get an idea of how others have approached this task, consider what Colleen, a young mother, wrote:

> I could relate so very well with this story. Ever since I can remember, I've been anxious about my appearance. I always worried about being too fat and spent way too much on clothes I didn't even wear. Then after I had the baby, I felt that he was getting all the attention and no one seemed to notice me any more.
>
> I realize now I'll never have the looks of a model, so I need to accept myself the way I am; but there are some things I can do. I need to exercise more and change my eating habits. I must try to remember to

ask God to free me from old ways of thinking.

Kathleen, a young artist, didn't come up with any special idea about what she might do to change her life. Instead, she came to a question that made her reconsider her worth. She wrote:

> I guess that because I'm a painter I see things that a lot of people don't. I love to do flowers, and I really did identify with Jesus' statement that even Solomon in his glory was not like one of these. Just to sit and look at the intricate designs in a flower is enough to awe me. And I wonder, Am I worth even more than that flower?

*   *   *

Use the remaining time to think about what God is helping you to realize about yourself. From what anxieties would you like to be freed? What steps can you take to bring more peace into your life? Write down your thoughts so you'll have something to look back on to see how you're growing spiritually.

Closing Prayer

(If you prefer, use an alternate prayer or psalm from Part Three, or pray the Lord's Prayer.)
O God, help me to understand that I'm only on a journey here in this world. When my days get cluttered and I feel anxious, show me ways to simplify my life. Help me to recognize how the quest for material possessions can become an obsession. Open my eyes to everything in nature that is wonder-full, so that I may be reminded of Jesus' teaching that I am worth more than all of that. I pray in Jesus' name. Amen.

Session 8

Turning Around

(Acts 22:3-16)

"Who are you, Lord?"

Creating the Environment

(5 minutes)
Take a few minutes to create a comfortable environment for your time alone with God. What you do depends on whether you're indoors or out, at home or away. If you're inside, do whatever is necessary to avoid being interrupted by the telephone or the doorbell. Get comfortable within your space by turning away from anything distracting and by setting up whatever will help you get into a proper frame of mind. You may want to open your Bible and place it within easy reach next to some flowers or a candle.

Will a picture of Jesus, a cross, a crucifix, or an icon help make you more aware of God's presence? If so, place your favored item near the Bible or wherever you can easily look at it without being distracted. Have at hand everything you may need, including your notebook and pens or pencils.

The objective is the same whether you are indoors or out—to be settled before going further.

Opening Prayer

O God, I thank you for sending Jesus into this world. I want to believe and to serve as Jesus commanded, but I have moments of doubt and weakness. Help me to review what I believe and to become aware of ways I must change in order to serve others more faithfully. Guide me to a deeper under- standing of whatever needs to be turned around in my life. I ask this in Jesus' name. Amen.

Silence

(10 minutes)
Set your timer.

The purpose of these ten minutes is to relax the body and prepare the mind and heart to become more attentive as you enter into a special time alone with God. Often when we first sit down, our minds are cluttered and we feel distracted. Don't fight your thoughts or focus long on those that come to mind. Instead, breathe deeply and evenly as you reflect on scripture. Use this line (Psalm 38:21) as a touchstone, and come back to it over and over as you remain silent:

O MY GOD, BE NOT FAR FROM ME!

Reading and Reflecting on Scripture

(25 minutes)
Set your timer.

The story for this session is the story of Saul's experience on the road to Damascus, which is found in Acts 22:3-16.

Read the story over and over. You may like to read it quietly and then again out loud. There is great power in the spoken word, even when it is your voice and you are the audience. You have almost half an hour, so there is no need to rush. When someting about the story strikes you, reflect on that idea. Be open to the Word and allow God's Spirit to lead your thoughts.

[Saul says,] "I am a Jew, born at Tarsus in Cilicia, but brought up in this city at the feet of Gamaliel, educated according to the strict manner of the law of our fathers, being zealous for God as you all are this day. I persecuted this Way to the death, binding and delivering to prison both men and women, as the high priest and the whole council of elders bear me witness. From them I received letters to the brethren, and I journeyed to Damascus to take those also who were there and bring them in bonds to Jerusalem to be punished.

"As I made my journey and drew near to Damascus, about noon a great light from heaven suddenly shone about me. And I fell to the ground and heard a voice saying to me, 'Saul, Saul, why do you persecute me?' And I answered, 'Who are you, Lord?' And he said to me, 'I am Jesus of Nazareth whom you are persecuting.' Now those who were with me saw the light but did not hear the voice of the one who was speaking to me. And I said, 'What shall I do, Lord?' And the Lord said to me, 'Rise, and go into Damascus, and there you will be told all that is appointed for you to do.' And when I could not see because of the brightness of that light, I was led by the hand by those who were with me, and came into Damascus.

"And one Ananias, a devout man according to the law, well spoken of by all the Jews who lived there, came to me, and standing by me said to me, 'Brother Saul, receive your sight.' And in that very hour I received my sight and saw him. And he said, 'The God of our fathers appointed you to know his will, to see the Just One and to hear a voice from his mouth; for you will be a witness for him to all men of what you have seen and heard. And now why do you wait? Rise and be baptized, and wash away your sins, calling on his name.'"

Another Dimension

(15 minutes)

Set your timer.

The purpose of this activity is to look at another dimension of the story.

The Acts of the Apostles includes two tellings (Chapters 9 and 22) of the story of Paul's conversion experience. The story is first told in a straightforward style we would expect in a newspaper report of the event. I find the second telling to be more useful because it is a personal account Paul uses in speaking before an audience.

What does Paul reveal about himself through his own account? He has reflected on his experience and recognizes that it is the foundation of both his ministry and his view of life in Jesus. This is an honest, straightforward testimony. Without fanfare or exaggeration, Paul tells who he is and what has happened to him. He offers no apologies for his past, but neither does he describe himself as being worse than he was. Paul makes it clear that he was acting out of ignorance and was not guilty of doing anything against God on purpose.

It's clear that despite his zealous actions, Paul's mind was not closed. He was definitely receptive to new ideas. We see how the question "Saul, Saul, why do you persecute me?" opened a whole new world, instead of leading to an argument or other defensive measure.

Paul, as Saul, had questions of his own. "Who are you, Lord?" he asks; and then comes the central statement that impels Paul forward throughout his life: "I am Jesus of Nazareth whom you are persecuting."

Again, there is an honest and touching response ("What shall I do, Lord?") that helps us understand how open the man was to whatever the Lord had to say.

At this point we might consider what our reaction would have been. Often when we feel that the Lord has spoken to us, we quickly decide on a course of action rather than waiting quietly for confirmation.

Paul's conversion experience involved not only a turning point in his life but also a profound insight into the meaning of community. Although Paul was zealous for God both before and after the experience that began on the road to Damascus, he changed in a very important way. He came to realize that those he had been persecuting were his companions in faith.

Paul's experience is one we all can have. We, too, can turn about from our old ways of thinking and acting to become more open to hearing the Lord identify with persecuted people.

Break/Rest/Walk

(15 minutes)
If you're feeling tired and need to rest, set your timer before lying down. If you're going for a walk, keep track of the time with your watch.

The purpose of this activity is to refresh yourself. Have a snack if you like, but whatever you do, continue to reflect in an easy way about Paul's experience.

Inner Dimension

(30 minutes)
Set your timer.

Get out your writing materials.

The purpose of this activity is to consider what we might be doing (in the name of a good cause) that is putting people down without our realizing it. We've seen that Saul, in his zeal, was persecuting others. It required a dramatic encounter for him to realize that he must change his ways.

Print these words at the top of a sheet of paper:

Family   Friends   Groups / Organizations

Now examine your actions and attitudes. Begin by considering your relationships within your immediate family. Perhaps some behavior that seems not only reasonable but good

to you needs to be "turned around." Think especially of those
things you're doing or saying to others that you believe are
"for their own good." Is it really the loving behavior you
think it is? Make notes to yourself under all three columns.

Review your actions and attitudes carefully, keeping in
mind Saul's hurtful zeal. We should question anything we're
doing expressely "for the good of" others; it may possibly be a
form of persecution.

Prayer of Response

(10 minutes)
Set your timer.

The purpose of this activity is to free you of distractions
and allow God to move quietly within your mind and heart.
All you need to do is sit still and return to this line (Psalm
54:2) whenever your attention wanders:

HEAR MY PRAYER, O GOD.

Reflection on Alonetime

(15 minutes)
Set your timer.

Get out your writing materials.

Now reflect on those habits and beliefs you take for
granted but which might require you to turn about in order
to experience a breakthrough in your spiritual life. What
you write in your notebook or journal must be personal and
honest. To get an idea of how others have approached this
task, consider the reflections of Laurie, who was attending a
technical school when she wrote:

Every time I hear the story about Saul on the road to
Damascus, I'm reminded of the way I grew up thinking
about religion. My parents always gave me the impression that our church was *the* church. They never really

said it, but I got the impression that we were better Christians than the people who belonged to other churches. It was like we were the chosen ones.

Then I went away to school and met lots of new people. Most of them came from other Christian denominations. Even though they seemed to practice their faith sincerely, I realize now that I did feel a little superior to them. I sort of let that idea float to the back of my mind. But now as I write about it, I see that I've got to do a lot of rethinking. I truly need to turn around from being so proud.

Sam was a sales person who held onto his way of doing things with the grip of a bulldog. There was only one way to look at any question, and that was Sam's way. It got so bad that he almost lost his job (and his family). But finally Sam had a breakthrough experience that turned his life around. This is what he wrote:

> I truly believed that if someone had not had my experience they *could not* be a real Christian. Paul's story helped me see that my problem was that I hadn't heard Jesus say, "Go and wait till I send someone to you." I went off preaching and proclaiming as if I knew it all.

Sam came to realize that he needed some quiet time to reconsider how Jesus was calling him. The turnabout came slowly, but Sam made it and—in time—became a much humbler man.

Now it's your turn to write. Reread what you wrote during the Inner Dimension activity. What is God helping you to see about yourself today? What behavior might God be calling you to turn from? Have you been blind to some aspect of your life that needs changing? How might you be called to make a breakthrough in some personal relationship?

Be as specific as you can, and try to think of three things you could begin to do immediately to continue to grow into the Lord's power and grace.

Closing Prayer
(If you prefer, use an alternate prayer or psalm from Part
Three, or pray the Lord's Prayer.)
O God of all creation, I thank you for life and for the chance to
turn about on whatever paths are not best for me. I've
reviewed my everyday habits; grant me the strength to turn
around whenever necessary and to seek a better path. I
realize that I don't always see you in other people. Please fill
me with power to understand the attitudes of others and
seek what is holy in them. I want to heal differences of
opinion and live rightly. I pray in Jesus' name. Amen.

Session 9

Called to Serve

(Exodus 3:1-12)

"Come, I will send you to Pharaoh
that you may bring forth my people. . . ."

Creating the Environment

(5 minutes)

Take a few minutes to create a comfortable environment for
your time alone with God. What you do depends on whether
you're indoors or out, at home or away. If you're inside, do
whatever is necessary to avoid being interrupted by the
telephone or the doorbell. Get comfortable within your space
by turning away from anything distracting and by setting
up whatever will help you get into a proper frame of mind.
You may want to open your Bible and place it within easy
reach next to some flowers or a candle.

Will a picture of Jesus, a cross, a crucifix, or an icon help
make you more aware of God's presence? If so, place your
favored item near the Bible or wherever you can easily look
at it without being distracted. Have at hand everything you
may need, including your notebook and pens or pencils.

The objective is the same whether you are indoors or
out—to be settled before going further.

Opening Prayer

God, I've put aside this time to be alone with you. I come

away from my daily routine wishing I could be on holy ground and sense your presence in my life in a new way. Help me to hear your voice during this time and come to a better understanding of the ministry I am called to. I pray in Jesus' name. Amen.

Silence

(10 minutes)
Set your timer.

The purpose of these ten minutes is to relax the body and prepare the mind and heart to become more attentive as you enter into a special time alone with God. Often when we first sit down, our minds are cluttered and we feel distracted. Don't fight your thoughts or focus long on those that come to mind. Instead, breathe deeply and evenly as you reflect on scripture. Use this line (Psalm 25:2) as a touchstone, and come back to it over and over as you remain silent:
O MY GOD, IN THEE I TRUST.

Reading and Reflecting on Scripture

(25 minutes)
Set your timer.

For this session of the series we look back to an ancient Old Testament story that speaks dramatically about God's voice in our lives. The story of the burning bush is found in Exodus 3:1-12.

Read the story over and over. You may like to read it quietly and than again out loud. There is great power in the spoken word, even when it is your voice and you are the audience. You have almost half an hour, so there is no need to rush. When something about the story strikes you, reflect on that idea. Be open to the Word and allow God to lead your thoughts.

Now Moses was keeping the flock of his father-in-law,
Jethro, the priest of Midian; and he led his flock to the

west side of the wilderness, and came to Horeb, the mountain of God. And the angel of the LORD appeared to him in a flame of fire out of the midst of a bush; and he looked, and lo, the bush was burning, yet it was not consumed. And Moses said, "I will turn aside and see this great sight, why the bush is not burnt." When the LORD saw that he turned aside to see, God called to him out of the bush, "Moses, Moses!" And he said, "Here am I." Then he said, "Do not come near; put off your shoes from your feet, for the place on which you are standing is holy ground." And he said, "I am the God of your father, the God of Abraham, the God of Isaac, and the God of Jacob." And Moses hid his face, for he was afraid to look at God.

Then the LORD said, "I have seen the affliction of my people who are in Egypt, and have heard their cry because of their taskmasters; I know their sufferings, and I have come down to deliver them out of the hands of the Egyptians, and to bring them up out of that land to a good and broad land, a land flowing with milk and honey, to the place of the Canaanites, the Hittites, and Amorites, the Perizzites, the Hivites, and the Jebusites. And now, behold, the cry of the people of Israel has come to me, and I have seen the oppression with which the Egyptians oppress them. Come, I will send you to Pharaoh that you may bring forth my people, the sons of Israel, out of Egypt." But Moses said to God, "Who am I that I should go to Pharoah, and bring the sons of Israel out of Egypt?" He said, "But I will be with you; and this shall be the sign for you, that I have sent you: when you have brought forth the people out of Egypt, you shall serve God upon this mountain."

Another Dimension

(15 minutes)
Set your timer.

The purpose of this activity is to look at another dimension of the story. In this case, we'll consider how the events that Moses experienced can help us to better understand what God reveals for us today. Although God calls in many ways, there is a pattern we can identify.

God calls us away from where we are. Usually God attracts our attention with something out of the ordinary. For us, the burning bush may be an event, a person, a statement, or even an unusual thought. What catches our attention is something or someone that touches us so deeply that we cannot shake it off.

We recognize that something is different and sense that it demands our pursuit on a personal level. The unusual event that captured our attention has an aura of mystery that seems to demand investigation and an explanation. Nowadays we have such a yearning to understand or "explain away" everything that we're in danger of losing our ability to appreciate the mysterious and our need for it.

We hear a call. We may "hear" God's call with our intuitive sense, or through a dream, or in some other way. Hearing the call doesn't necessarily mean we will hear it with our ears, but we might. It's important to be attentive because we're in danger of losing our ability to recognize and appreciate the mysterious. Most of us have fewer and fewer moments of quiet reflection, and some younger people are so plugged into sound that they may have completely lost the ability to listen for anything mysterious.

We answer. We can, of course, pretend to ignore everything about the burning-bush experience, but some aspect of it will continue to come back to us. It may be that we, like Moses, hide our face when we recognize that we are in God's presence. Eventually, though, Moses responded to the call. Can we do less?

Finally, *we receive a commission to ministry.* The experience of the burning bush is always a commission to do something with or for others. It's a mistake to consider the experience as being strictly for ourselves.

For the people with whom I've worked who were trying to find a way through their own burning-bush encounters, God's call to ministry has always been a calling forth of strengths or skills from our past. That is, everything that has happened up to the time of the call is preparation—necessary preparation. If we look again to Moses, we see that his knowledge of both the Hebrew and Egyptian worlds suited him for the task he was to fulfill. It is the same with us.

If you have time, reread the story with these ideas in mind.

Break/Rest/Walk

(15 minutes)
If you're feeling tired and need to rest, set your timer before lying down. If you're going for a walk, keep track of the time with your watch.

The purpose of this activity is to refresh yourself. Have a snack if you like, but whatever you do, continue to reflect in an easy way about the story of Moses and the burning bush.

Inner Dimension

(30 minutes)
Set your timer.

The purpose of this activity is to review your own life in order to better understand what God has been preparing you for.

Every one of us has a story to tell about a burning bush. Perhaps you're already thinking about a particular experience in your life and are ready to put it down on paper. Or you may feel the need to ponder awhile. In either case, it's helpful to see examples from the lives of others.

Martin had been a minister for a number of years. Everything was going well for him. But he did have a sense of unease that he expressed openly:

I guess I've come to learn that whenever I get to

feeling a little uncomfortable, that's a sign to be alert. One day I was reading in a church magazine and found myself going through the Positions Wanted & Needed section. I didn't remember ever having read that section before, but there I was giving it full attention. All of a sudden one four-line ad appeared like a neon sign. It shocked me so that I put the magazine aside.

An hour later, I came back to the ad, and it was like the letters were four feet tall! Needless to say, I applied for the position and got it. I see now that it was exactly what I had been preparing for for years. I haven't told this to many people, because I'm sure they'd think I was looney.

Donna, a mother of teenagers, had a similar experience, but in her case it was brought about by another person. Donna said:

I was at a weekend retreat and everything was going well. Then out of the blue I was handed a note from someone I knew at home. She said she was praying for me while I was on retreat. As I read that note, it was like a fire consuming me. I couldn't understand what was happening. It was as though a whole new world of God's power opened up to me. I was struck with awe and began crying joyfully. I recognized that I was on holy ground.

Accustomed to working under pressure as a business consultant, John had not thought much about his spiritual life. When he became aware of the idea that we all have a burning-bush experience at some time, he began to pay more attention to the possibility that God's time and our time do intersect. John explained:

I was overseeing a conference of five people who got into a heated discussion. It was my job to observe the process in order to reflect back to them some of the causes of their office problems. One of the men suddenly said, "I don't want to talk about it any more. We're getting nowhere."

There was an embarrassing silence.

I had an immediate awareness that there was a power present that I couldn't explain. I heard myself saying, "I have a sense we're on holy ground. And in the midst of the mystery of trying to understand the problem, we're nearly at the resolution and the revelation of it."

It was odd. I'd never said anything like that before. The others looked at me and seemed to sense something different at that moment as well. A resolution came quickly after that. God's power was at work in my work.

*   *   *

Now get out your writing materials.

Spend the remainder of your time recalling what you can about a moment in your life when you felt you were on holy ground, a moment when you were having a burning-bush experience.

When did it happen?

What was your immediate reaction?

How do you feel about the experience now?

Prayer of Response

(10 minutes)

Set your timer.

Get our your writing materials.

Now review the special moment or moments when you felt you were on holy ground, and see if you can discover to what ministry you have been called. Although the direction may not be immediately clear, each experience of being on holy ground is a call to minister to others in some particular way. To get an idea how others have approached this task, consider what Larry, a former drinker who now counsels other alcoholics, wrote:

> I didn't know what I wanted to do with my life. I drifted from one job to another, and it seemed the only thing I knew how to do well was drink. As the years went on, it reached the point where just about everybody gave up on me.
>
> I see now that even the worst things that happened to me can have some value. God had something useful for me to do. I was just too stubborn to see that for a long, long time.
>
> It's still a revelation to me that God should be so patient!

* * *

Now it's your turn to write. What has God been revealing to you that you can now admit to yourself? Are you called to head a group? Adopt a problem child? Join a cause? Turn your back on some destructive behavior and use your knowledge to help others? Is God telling you to change your profession? Renew your commitment to marriage?

God is calling, but only you can answer. Look deeply and honestly at yourself. Make notes in your journal, and outline the steps you know you should take in response to the burning-bush experience, or experiences, in your life.

Closing Prayer

(If you prefer, use an alternate prayer or psalm from Part Three, or pray the Lord's Prayer.)

O God, I realize that you called Moses at a time when he least expected it. Is the same thing happening to me? As I grow older, I want to understand what you've been preparing me for. Help me to be aware of the holy ground you place before me. Open my ears that I may hear, and open my heart to appreciate the ministry to which you call me. I pray in Jesus' name. Amen.

Part Three

Prayers

This section contains additional prayers that you may use in place of those written into the sessions or as prayers throughout the day.

We all have our individual ways of praying just as we have our individual ways of talking. I've included prayers and psalms to help you whether you are accustomed to speaking with God formally or informally. Some are meant to be used at specific times such as morning, noon, evening, and end of the day, but others may be used whenever they seem suitable.

Christian history includes a tradition of praying several times during the day. In the past, when the rhythm of life was more set, prayer patterns were also more set. People prayed especially in the morning, again at noontime, in the late afternoon, and finally just before going to sleep.

Whatever your customary approach to prayer is, there are some prayers in this section that you'll be comfortable using during your time alone with God. Besides the formal prayers (which follow the general pattern of "official" prayers of many denominations), there are shorter, informal ones, as well as a few specific prayers to use both in times of stress or discomfort and in times of great joy and thankfulness.

Do you find yourself feeling too rushed to pray at noon or at any time later in the day? If so, that's not unusual. However, the very busy-ness that makes us skip prayer time may be all the more reason to pray. Sharing a few thoughts

with God may be the very thing needed to get us through a
busy afternoon successfully. If you have to face the demands
of children at home, the pressure of a business meeting, the
need to get important studying done, or any of a hundred
other stressful activities, *make time* for prayer on a regular
basis. Make time at noon and later in the afternoon as well.
Pray just before the kids come home from school or at the end
of your coffeebreak. Pray while you're headed home after
work, or right after supper and before you begin your evening activities. Pick a time that will be available on any
average day, and try to make praying at that time as much of
a habit as eating.

If your prayer life has become a bit lax (no matter what the
reason), make a commitment during one of your alone-with-
God sessions to get back in the habit. Pray morning, midday,
afternoon, and end of the day prayers regularly *for three
weeks,* and the discipline will become very natural for you.
Try it. You're likely to find that at the end of that time
missing a prayer will be like missing a meal.

IN THE MORNING

Introduction

Come, bless the LORD, all you servants of the
      LORD!

                                              (Psalm 134:1)

Psalm

Praise the LORD.
   I will give thanks to the LORD with my whole
      heart,
   in the company of the upright, in the
      congregation.
Great are the works of the LORD,

studied by all who have pleasure in them.
Full of honor and majesty is his work,
    and his righteousness endures for ever.
He has caused his wonderful works to be
        remembered;
    the LORD is gracious and merciful.
He provides food for those who fear him;
    he is ever mindful of his covenant.
He has shown his people the power of his works,
    in giving them the heritage of the nations.
The works of his hands are faithful and just;
    all his precepts are trustworthy,
they are established for ever and ever,
    to be performed with faithfulness and
        uprightness.
He sent redemption to his people;
    he has commanded his covenant for ever.
Holy and terrible* is his name!
The fear** of the LORD is the beginning of
        wisdom;
    a good understanding have all those who
        practice it.
His praise endures for ever!

(Psalm 111)

Response

For my life . . . I praise you, loving Creator.

For the newly created day and opportunity . . . I praise
you, loving Creator.

For all the people who love me, and all those who find it

---

*Our English version may make it difficult for us to understand the
richness of meaning the psalmist is attempting to convey. The writer
wants the reader to realize that the very name of the Lord ought to fill
us with a combination of wonder, awe, respect and love.
**We might better understand "fear" in this context to mean "respect-
filled love."

hard to love me . . . I praise you, loving Creator.
    For Jesus Christ . . . I praise you, loving Creator.

Scripture Reading

"Then, turning to the disciples he said privately, 'Blessed
are the eyes which see what you see! For I tell you that
many prophets and kings desired to see what you see, and
did not see it, and to hear what you hear, and did not hear
it.' " (Luke 10:23-24)

Prayer

O God, you are a mighty creator and sustainer of the
world. You placed me in the midst of your creation that I
might see your goodness and praise your mighty works.
Grant me the insight to continue to foster the right use
and protection of the earth, that all may be brought into
the fullness of the light of the world, your Son, our Lord,
Jesus. Amen.

Silent Time for Personal Intercessions

The Lord's Prayer

Blessing

May the Lord God who placed me in the midst of this
creation fill me with his powerful Spirit. Amen.

MIDDAY PRAYER

Introduction

As the sun is high in the sky, may I stand in the brightness
of your light, O God.

Psalm

May God be gracious to us and bless us,
　and make his face to shine upon us
that thy way may be known upon earth,
　thy saving power among all nations.
Let the peoples praise thee, O God;
　let all the peoples praise thee!

Let the nations be glad and sing for joy,
　for thou dost judge the peoples with equity
　and guide the nations upon earth.

Let the peoples praise thee, O God;
　let all the peoples praise thee!

The earth has yielded its increase;
　God, our God, has blessed us.
God has blessed us;
　let all the ends of the earth fear him!

(Psalm 67)

Prayer

I acclaim you, gracious Lord, for all your mighty gifts. You provide me with bread and drink day by day. You cover me with your wings of protection within my home. Open my eyes to see more clearly your power in our midst, that all those I know may come to an ever greater understanding of your love. Grant that as I come to appreciate your love more and more, I may be a reminder for others that you are gracious to your people. I pray in Jesus' name. Amen.

Scripture Reading

"Therefore I tell you, do not be anxious about your life, what you shall eat or what you shall drink, nor about your body, what you shall put on. Is not life more than food, and the body more than clothing? Look at the birds of the air: they neither sow nor reap nor gather into barns, and yet

your heavenly Father feeds them. Are you not of more
value than they?" (Matthew 6:25-26)

Silence for Reflecting on
How The Word Relates to Your Life

Intercessions

> For all who are homeless . . . I pray in trust, O
> Provider.
> For all who are hungry . . . I pray in trust, O
> Provider.
> For all who are at war . . . I pray in trust, O
> Provider.
> For all who seek truth and justice . . . I pray in
> trust, O Provider.
> For all people whose lives I touch . . . I pray in
> trust, O Provider.

The Lord's Prayer

Blessing

As God makes his sun to shine on the earth, may he make
his face shine upon me. Amen.

EVENING PRAYER

Introduction

At the setting of the sun, may the Lord be blessed!

Psalm

> Praise the LORD!
> Praise, O servants of the LORD,
>   praise the name of the LORD!
>
> Blessed be the name of the LORD

from this time forth and for evermore!
From the rising of the sun to its setting
   the name of the LORD is to be praised!
The LORD is high above all nations,
   and his glory above the heavens!

Who is like the LORD our God,
   who is seated on high,
who looks far down
   upon the heavens and the earth?
He raises the poor from the dust,
   and lifts the needy from the ash heap,
to make them sit with princes,
   with the princes of his people.
He gives the barren woman a home,
   making her the joyous mother of children.
Praise the LORD!

(Psalm 113)

Response

For all the times I have been forgiven . . . may the
   Lord be blessed.
For my friends and family . . . may the Lord be
   blessed.
For the times I have felt God's presence . . . may the
   Lord be blessed.
For this time of prayer . . . may the Lord be blessed.

Scripture Reading

"Again, the kingdom of heaven is like a net which was
thrown into the sea and gathered fish of every kind; when
it was full, men drew it ashore and sat down and sorted the
good into vessels but threw away the bad." (Matthew
13:47-48)

Prayer

God, as I come to the evening of this day, grant that I may see more clearly the good and the bad elements of my life. Lead me to a greater understanding of the importance of decisions I make each day. Grant that I may be a symbol of the kingdom of heaven to those people I already know and those I am about to meet. I ask this in the name of Jesus, your son. Amen.

Silent Time for Personal Intercessions

The Lord's Prayer

Blessing

May the Spirit that filled this day with life and new opportunities continue to fill this evening and night with the power of God's love. Amen.

PRAYER AT DAY'S END

Introduction

Blessed be the God of the heavens, of the sun and of the moon.

Psalm

> Come, bless the LORD,
>> all you servants of the LORD,
>> who stand by night in the house of the LORD!
> Lift up your hands to the holy place,
>> and bless the LORD!
>
> May the LORD bless you from Zion,
>> he who made heaven and earth!
>
> (Psalm 134)

Silence for Intercessions

Scripture Reading

Now may the God of peace who brought again from the dead our Lord Jesus, the great shepherd of the sheep, by the blood of the eternal covenant, equip you with everything good that you may do his will, working in you that which is pleasing in his sight, through Jesus Christ; to whom be glory for ever and ever. Amen. (Hebrews 13:20-21)

Silence for Confession of Your Faults of This Day

Prayer

"Lord, now lettest thou thy servant depart in peace, according to thy word; for mine eyes have seen thy salvation which thou has prepared in the presence of all peoples, a light for revelation to the Gentiles, and for glory to thy people Israel." (Luke 2:29-32)

Blessing

May the Lord grant me a peaceful night and give strength to those who work while I sleep.

MORNING PRAYER

God,
at the beginning of this new day
I give thanks to you with my whole heart.
For my life . . . I praise you.
For the newly created day
and the opportunity it may bring . . . I praise you.
For all my friends . . . I praise you.
Grant me patience and understanding, and
may your ever-present love be felt by those I know.
Today, I ask especially that you bless

_____(my spouse, boss, child, neighbor)_____.
Amen.

MIDDAY PRAYER

In the middle of this busy day,
I turn to you, God, with hope in heart.
I look at the birds of the air who neither sow nor reap
and try to understand that you care for them
and you care for me.
Caring God, I am grateful for all my blessings,
but I continue to need your help.
Open my eyes so that I see more clearly
how your love may come to life through me
as I go about my business this afternoon.
Amen.

EVENING PRAYER

O God, it has been a busy day
and I need to feel your comforting presence.
Refresh me so that I might
be patient with those I love.
Amen.

PRAYER AT DAY'S END

Now, at the end of my day, I place my trust in you, Lord.
Be present to all those people who are important to me
especially _____(names)_____.
Forgive me for whatever hurts I have caused,
strengthen the belief that lies within my heart,
and grant me a restful sleep.
Amen.

PRAYER FOR FORGIVENESS

God of all creation, I ask pardon for my faults,
for all the times when I have said or thought or done
things harmful to myself or others.
I regret those times when through negligence
I did not do, think, or say what would have helped.
Forgive me as I forgive others who have harmed me.
I ask to be forgiven in Jesus' name.
Amen.

PRAYER OF PRAISE TO GOD

For all those who love me, I praise you, God.
For this time alone, I praise you.
For all those who have been my teachers, I praise you.
For the beauty of sun and sky, I praise you.
For my mind and all it can do, I praise you.
For life and love, I praise you.
Amen.

PRAYER OF GRIEF

Dear God, death is hard to understand.
I feel anger, I feel pain.
I feel numb, I feel empty.
I feel love lost.
I do not sleep well. I do not eat well.
Dear God, death is hard to understand.
I feel no joy, I feel no hope.
I feel no future, I feel no past.
I only feel love lost.
Dear God, death is hard to understand.
Help me survive the pain of loss.
I pray in Jesus' name. Amen.

PRAYER FOR PATIENCE

Being patient is not one of my strengths. I know that.
Everyone who knows me knows that. Today I don't even
have patience to pray! God, please help me sit quietly,
breathe deeply, and be patient. Amen.

PRAYER FOR STUDENTS

God, I need someone to talk to. She isn't in school today,
and there are lots of rumors going round. People say she
tried to kill herself. Nobody seems to have any details.
And nobody seems to know why. She was very quiet. I
never got to know her well. I'd just say "Hi" to her in the
halls. Sat next to her a few times at lunch. She seemed OK.
But it bothers me. Suppose I'd done more than say "Hi."
Could it have made a difference? This school is full of quiet
kids. I can't get close to all of them. Probably they've all
got problems. But I'm just one person. Still, there's this
one kid I've noticed. He's pretty down. Think I'll grab the
seat next to him on the bus today. Kind of get acquainted
and let him know there're friends around. God, I guess you
know I just have to talk to you sometimes. Thanks for
listening. Amen.

PRAYER OF HOPE

O God, I have a song to sing. Help me sing it. I have a
dream to make real. Help me to do it. I have myself to be.
Help me to be all that I can be. And if I stop singing, or
forget my dreams, help me to begin again with hope.
Amen.

PRAYER FOR BELIEF

God of wind and setting sun,
God of babies crying and kids playing,

God of my best dreams,
I want to believe.
I want my belief to be something
that encourages me to grow.
I want my belief to be something
that guides me toward finding meaning in life.
I seek a faith to free me to live, not just exist.
Dear God, this is my prayer—help me to believe.
Amen.

PRAYER FOR THE SICK

God, Creator of life, you know that I don't handle sickness
very well. Help those who are like me and get sick of being
sick in no time at all. Inspire nurses and doctors to have
compassion and listen to patients who need a friendly
word as much as medicine. Guide visitors to the homes of
the bedridden who feel forgotten. Bestow patience on anyone who suffers alone. Help me to be faithful to my beliefs
in times of sickness as well as times of health. I pray in the
name of Jesus, who suffered and died that we might live.
Amen.

PRAYER FOR THE DIVORCED

God, will I ever understand?
I believed in marriage, gave to it what I could.
Still, it has ended.
There is pain. And anger. And fear.
There has never been a time in my life
when I felt such a need for someone to love me.
Please, take away my sense of failure.
Please, let me sense your presence in my life,
and help me to feel worthy once again.
Amen.

PRAYER FOR FAMILIES

I love my family, God, and miss them when I'm away.
I pray that you watch over and protect not only my family
but all families.
I pray especially for troubled people.
Where there is abuse, bring change.
Where there is infidelity, restore faithful love.
Where there is yelling, inspire calm.
Where there is alienation, reunite people.
Make us all more sensitive to one another's needs
so that we may reach out in love to create strong families
and wise people.
Amen.

PSALM 4

Answer me when I call, O God of my right!
    Thou hast given me room when I was in
        distress.
    Be gracious to me, and hear my prayer.

O men, how long shall my honor suffer shame?
    How long will you love vain words, and seek
        after lies?
But know that the LORD has set apart the godly
    for himself;
    the LORD hears when I call to him.

Be angry, but sin not;
    commune with your own hearts on your beds,
        and be silent.
Offer right sacrifices,
    and put your trust in the LORD.

There are many who say, "O that we might see
    some good!
    Lift up the light of thy countenance upon us, O
    LORD!"

Thou hast put more joy in my heart
  than they have when their grain and wine
    abound.

In peace I will both lie down and sleep;
  for thou alone, O LORD, makest me dwell in
    safety.

PSALM 46

God is our refuge and strength
  a very present help in trouble.
Therefore we will not fear though the earth
    should change,
    though the mountains shake in the heart of the
      sea;
though its waters roar and foam,
    though the mountains tremble with its tumult.

There is a river whose streams make glad the city
    of God,
    the holy habitation of the Most High.
God is in the midst of her, she shall not be moved;
  God will help her right early.
The nations rage, the kingdoms totter;
  he utters his voice, the earth melts.
The LORD of hosts is with us;
  the God of Jacob is our refuge.

Come, behold the works of the LORD,
  how he has wrought desolations in the earth.
He makes wars cease to the end of the earth;
  he breaks the bow, and shatters the spear,
  he burns the chariots with fire!
"Be still, and know that I am God.
  I am exalted among the nations,
  I am exalted in the earth!"

The LORD of hosts is with us;
   the God of Jacob is our refuge.

PSALM 61

Hear my cry, O God,
   listen to my prayer;
from the end of the earth I call to thee,
   when my heart is faint.

Lead thou me
   to the rock that is higher than I;
for thou art my refuge,
   a strong tower against the enemy.

Let me dwell in thy tent for ever!
   Oh to be safe under the shelter of thy wings!
For thou, O God, hast heard my vows,
   thou hast given me the heritage of those who
      fear thy name.

Prolong the life of the king;
   may his years endure to all generations!
May he be enthroned for ever before God;
   bid steadfast love and faithfulness watch over
      him!

So will I ever sing praises to thy name,
   as I pay my vows day after day.

PSALM 121

I lift up my eyes to the hills.
   From whence does my help come?
My help comes from the LORD,
   who made heaven and earth.

He will not let your foot be moved,
   he who keeps you will not slumber.

Behold, he who keeps Israel
  will neither slumber nor sleep.

The LORD is your keeper;
  the LORD is your shade
  on your right hand.
The sun shall not smite you by day,
  nor the moon by night.

The LORD will keep you from all evil;
  he will keep your life.
The LORD will keep
  your going out and your coming in
  from this time forth and for evermore.

Afterword

Never Really Alone

A time comes when the retreat must end. Whether we've been alone with God for two hours or two days, something unusual has happened. God's Spirit has breathed on us. Perhaps some doors that were closed have been opened to reveal not only a need to change but also a way to change. We may have felt the wondrous release of being forgiven or sensed a peacefulness we'd like to hold onto forever.

At all the retreats I have the privilege to take part in, there's a moment when the participants gather just before setting off for home. Inevitably someone says, "Well, it's time to go back to the real world." There is an unspoken thought that God is active only in the quiet, alone times we have.

Wherever you may be as you end your own retreat, be thankful for the quiet time, but do not leave feeling that the *real* times of prayer are when you are alone behind a closed door, isolated in the woods, or sitting quietly by yourself in a chapel. Such moments are spiritually rich because we are freed of the usual distractions. It's not unusual under such circumstances to become so committed to being alone with God that we think God is alone with us. This place where we've had such a good experience is certainly not the only place where God is active! And, despite the feelings we may have had, we are not God's only partners. God is God of the universe and beyond. God is God of all—those we love and those we do not love.

Although we are invited to take our time alone with God and be strengthened by the experience, we must also be in the world as Jesus was and be aware that God is present in *all* times and *all* places. Few of us are born to be hermits who could, or should, live in prayerful isolation. Indeed, most of us are called to listen, touch other lives, and heal right within the boundaries of our own communities. Of course, as people of faith we are nourished by retreats and thus better prepared to proclaim justice and peace.

We are called to proclaim the same Spirit of God as Jesus did when he began his ministry. In a Nazareth synagogue on a Sabbath day, Jesus read these words aloud from the book of the prophet Isaiah:

"The Spirit of the Lord is upon me,
> because he has anointed me to preach good
> > news to the poor.
> He has sent me to proclaim release to the
> > captives
> and recovering of sight to the blind,
> to set at liberty those who are oppressed,
> to proclaim the acceptable year of the LORD."
> > > > > > (Luke 4:18-19)

The direction of a personal ministry, which we touched on in Session 9, may remain the same or change from year to year and even from month to month! By taking alonetime, you not only praise and glorify God but also have the opportunity to reflect on just how you're being nourished by the gift of God's love and what that gift is preparing you to do.

Through your experience of alonetime, you've been prepared to have life more abundantly. So go forth, ready to respond with love to the people closest to you, the people with whom you live and work and play. These are the people with whom you and I must continue planting the seeds of peace and justice that we would like to see grow around the world.

Go forth, rejoicing in the power of the Holy Spirit!